THE
MEAT
MARKET

THE
MEAT
MARKET
THE INSIDE STORY OF
THE NFL DRAFT

Richard Whittingham

MACMILLAN PUBLISHING COMPANY
New York

MAXWELL MACMILLAN CANADA
Toronto

MAXWELL MACMILLAN INTERNATIONAL
New York   Oxford   Singapore   Sydney

Macmillan Publishing Company   Maxwell Macmillan Canada, Inc.
866 Third Avenue   1200 Eglinton Avenue East
New York, NY 10022   Suite 200
                                 Don Mills, Ontario M3C 3N1

Macmillan Publishing Company is part of the Maxwell Communication Group of Companies.

Library of Congress Cataloging-in-Publication Data
Whittingham, Richard, date.
    The meat market: the inside story of the NFL draft/Richard Whittingham.
        p.   cm.
    Includes index.
    ISBN 0-02-627662-3
    1. Football—United States—Draft.   2. Football players—United States—Recruiting.   3. National Football League.   I. Title.
GV954.32.W47   1992   92-13411   CIP
796.332'64'0973—dc20

Designed by Michael Mendelsohn of M 'N O Production Services, Inc.

10   9   8   7   6   5   4   3   2   1

Printed in the United States of America

Contents

Acknowledgments

The author and publisher would like to express their deep appreciation to the Chicago Bear organization for its help and guidance while this book was being developed, especially president and CEO Michael McCaskey; vice president of player personnel Bill Tobin; scouts Rod Graves, Jim Parmer, and Don King; and all the others who sat for interviews and answered a plethora of questions.

Special thanks are also extended to Rick Korch, managing editor of *Pro Football Weekly,* for his most helpful assistance; to Joe Horrigan, pro football historian and archives curator of the Pro Football Hall of Fame in Canton, Ohio, for all his help; and to agent-entrepreneur Jack Childers, for his initiation and support of this project.

THE
MEAT
MARKET

1

D-DAY

Springtime.

Baseball season has started, pro basketball is still in full swing, hockey's Stanley Cup playoffs are under way. But this week in mid-April 1991, the sports pages are filled with stories about football—pro football—and the sports talk on radio and television is much the same. It is the week bearing down on the National Football League draft—D-Day.

As John Madden, former coach and now TV football analyst, put it in his literary meander, *Hey Wait a Minute, I Wrote a Book*: "Except for the day of a big game, the best day in pro football is the day the NFL teams draft college players." And former NFL commissioner Pete Rozelle corroborated: "It [the NFL draft] has become a major publicity tool. . . . There's a great curiosity and inasmuch as it covers the entire country so heavily—the colleges plus the NFL teams—it's a major promotional event. The draft is probably second only to the Super Bowl."

In 1991, D-Day is Sunday, April 21, when the first four rounds will be conducted, and Monday, April 22, for the fifth through twelfth rounds.

In New York, in the Broadway Ballroom on the sixth floor of

the Marriott Marquis Hotel at Broadway and 46th Street, the stage is set. There is a head table of sorts at which sit Paul Tagliabue, the NFL commissioner, and a passel of other NFL officials, with the podium and microphone standing ready next to it. Facing it are rows of tables where representatives of the twenty-eight NFL teams sit with their direct-line telephones, notepads, and other paraphernalia. There is a gallery of pro football aficionados observing the whole scene who know just as much as the player personnel directors and scouts.

There are hundreds of thousands who will tune in to ESPN cable television, which will carry the draft live throughout the day, or who will listen to it on radio stations in all the major cities of the United States. These are the die-hard fans of the game. They play Fantasy Football; they follow every aspect of the game (stats, prospects, injuries, team needs, team not-needs); they have definite opinions of how the draft will go—and how it should have gone once the choices have been made.

In twenty-eight cities throughout the United States, war rooms, as they are called, are staffed and press/media rooms are filled to capacity at the various team headquarters. At noon, Eastern Standard Time, the timer will be set in motion and D-Day will officially begin. The Dallas Cowboys, who the previous Friday traded up with the New England Patriots (which in NFL jargon means they traded for a higher draft choice), will then have the prescribed fifteen minutes to make the first selection in the first round of the 1991 NFL college football draft.

In Lake Forest, Illinois, at the headquarters of the Chicago Bears, Halas Hall—named for the team's founder, George Halas, the winningest coach in NFL history (326 wins, 151 losses, and 31 ties in regular-season games) and the man often referred to as the father of professional football—the day begins early.

As early as 7:30, cars are making their way through the tree-lined, gaslit streets of one of Chicago's most exclusive suburbs—where mailboxes in front of the sprawling mansions contain names like Armour, Swift, Wrigley, McCormick, and others of old-line wealth—to the parking lot of Halas Hall on the picturesque campus of Lake Forest College.

Some of the scouts have come early, to go over their notes, to review the mock drafts they have held during the preceding week, to recheck the grades that have been given to the "meat" at each position. They are upstairs in the war room, off-limits to all but a very select few. Bill Tobin, vice president of player personnel, is in his office just off the war room. Most of his time is spent on the telephone, talking to other teams about trade possibilities and getting information on trades that will affect the rotation of picks in the draft.

The Bears' public relations people also arrive early and head downstairs to the large press/media room, which ordinarily serves as a team meeting room, to be sure everything is in order for the throng of sportswriters from the *Chicago Tribune*, the *Chicago Sun-Times*, the wire services, and many of the suburban newspapers, and the cameramen, technicians, and broadcasters who will be covering the event for television and radio. Others are also downstairs across from the press/media room setting up the coffee, juice, sweet rolls, and cups of yogurt to satisfy the morning cravings of these guests of the Bears, who will be arriving around nine o'clock.

The press kits, containing everything from a comprehensive history of previous Bear drafts to preprinted forms that will allow the 1991 draft to be easily charted, are laid out in neat piles. Special telephones have already been installed, as have electrical outlets and special wiring to satisfy the needs of the audiovisual school of sports journalism.

Upstairs, the war room is ready, and has been for a week. Stepping into the room, one cannot miss the sign, the old World War II maxim:

LOOSE LIPS SINK SHIPS

One wall is papered with the names of players for each position, vertical rows of magnetic strips. At the top of each row is the highest-rated player at his position according to the Bears' system of grading, which is the result of a combination of things. Among the considerations that led to the ratings are Bill Tobin's grading; information received from the Bear scouts and from BLESTO, the scouting combine to which the Bears subscribe; and information gleaned from the NFL's National Invitational Camp for potential draftees, held a few months earlier. All of the information has been organized and assessed at team headquarters and a final grade has been given by Tobin. Next to each name is the Bear grading, which can range from 0.0, the highest, to 4.1, the lowest. The names descend in order of grading: from top fullback to lowest-graded fullback, top safety to lowest-graded safety . . .

There are approximately five hundred names of college football players on the lists on that wall; a few weeks earlier the lists contained about a thousand names.

The players' college affiliations are duly noted with each name, a lot of the players representing Michigan, Alabama, Florida, Notre Dame, Nebraska, Penn State, Southern Cal . . . the big time. But there are also kids from Baylor and Bucknell, Georgia Southern and Idaho State, even Towson State, Jackson State, Weber State, Ball State, and Prairie View A & M. In the 1990s, no player of any significance is overlooked.

On another wall there are twenty-eight vertical lists, each under a name of one of the twenty-eight NFL teams. These are the charts where draftees, as they are selected by each team, will be logged.

The conference table sits in the middle of the room. There is the direct-line telephone to the Bear representative at draft headquarters in New York—Ken Mrock, the team's groundskeeper. Groundskeeper? It is not uncommon for teams in the NFL to have unusual personnel manning the telephones at draft headquarters—Vince Lombardi used to have a friend who was a high school coach in New Jersey represent the Packers every D-Day; other teams have sent assistant trainers, equipment managers, and other assorted club employees. With Mrock is Dan Gleason—a friend, so to speak, of the Bear family who lives on Long Island. Gleason has been manning the desk at draft headquarters in New York with a representative from the Bear front office since the Jim Finks days in the mid-1970s. You need two people, Tobin advises, because one of them has to be at the New York end of the open line at all times and there are things that come up, like bathroom breaks.

There are additional open-line telephones to talk trades with other teams. There is the library of potential-draftee biographies collected from Bear scouting reports, BLESTO, and sundry other sources.

D-Day is an appropriate name. The day of the NFL draft has all the elements of the famous World War II invasion of the beaches of Normandy. All three of the basic elements of military intelligence—collection of information, dissemination of it, and evaluation of it, so basic they are in the forewords to the CIA, KGB, and Mossad manuals—have been meticulously taken care of. Security is as tight surrounding the war room here as it is in the basement of the Pentagon, and has been the entire week preceding the draft.

Everything has been carefully prepared by a troop of workers. The only thing that awaits is the action itself. It is, in the words of Gil Brandt, the legendary player personnel director of the Dallas Cowboys throughout the entire Tom Landry/Tex Schramm era, "kind of like Christmas morning when you have a family of little kids and everybody is about to start opening presents."

Nine o'clock in the morning, Central Standard Time. Everyone is assembling at Halas Hall. Bill Tobin, who is kind of the Norman

5

Schwarzkopf of this operation, is in and out of the war room, in and out of his office. Despite his graying hair, his boyish good looks belie the fact that Tobin is fifty years old. He is intense, introspective; he is the man who brings together all the information, determines the final Bear grade for each prospect, and orchestrates all aspects that lead up to the event that is about to transpire in the Bear war room.

Tobin has been with the Bears for seventeen years, but he has been around football on a serious level since his college days at the University of Missouri, where he was a star running back. After a stint with the Houston Oilers in 1963, where he won club Rookie of the Year honors, he moved on to the Edmonton Eskimos in the Canadian Football League and then to the Orlando Panthers franchise in the Continental Football League.

Prior to joining the Bears, Tobin was a regional scout for the Green Bay Packers for several years and then their director of pro scouting for another two years. One could say he got off on the right foot in 1975 in his first year with the Bears as director of pro scouting—the team's first-round draft pick that year was running back Walter Payton of Jackson State. That year the Bears also drafted quarterback Bob Avellini, safety Doug Plank, defensive end Mike Hartenstine, cornerback Virgil Livers, guard Revie Sorey, linebacker Tom Hicks, and fullback Roland Harper, all of whom went on to have long and productive careers with the Bears.

In his seventeen years of participation in the draft for the Bears, all nineteen of the club's top draft picks have been effective players and thirteen are still active in the NFL. Overall, fourteen Bear draft choices and two free agents since 1980 have made the Pro Bowl.

Under Tobin, the Bears' roster has been built almost exclusively through the draft. Thirty-nine of the team's forty-nine players in 1991 were Bear draftees and ten were signed as free agents.

He has a lot on his mind this morning.

Michael McCaskey, president and CEO of the organization,

6

walks in and sits down at the head of the conference table. He has held that title since 1983, when he succeeded his grandfather, Papa Bear Halas. McCaskey, who has a Ph.D. in business and who taught at UCLA and the Harvard School of Business, ran a business consulting company before taking over the Bear reins. He is a hands-on CEO. He is integrally involved in all facets of the team's operation, and he loves it.

When McCaskey first met the media as the Bears' CEO, he stated his goal: "That the Bears, year after year, be one of the best teams in football and that they win the Super Bowl." And the Bears soon became one of the NFL's premier teams. In the seven years preceding the 1991 season, the Bears have maintained the second-best record in the NFL, won six division titles, made three appearances in the NFC championship game, and won Super Bowl XX, defeating the New England Patriots by what was in January 1986 the largest margin in Super Bowl history, 46–10 (the 49ers outdid the Bears four years later when they annihilated the Broncos 55–10 in Super Bowl XXIV).

In the war room, McCaskey talks amiably with the scouts; all of them have arrived by this time.

Jim Parmer, who used to play in the backfield with Steve Van Buren in the Philadelphia Eagles' heyday, has been on the Bears' staff for nineteen years and is essentially considered the dean emeritus of Bear scouts. Parmer these days covers only Texas and Louisiana, but in years past he also covered the Midwest and Southwest for the Bears as well. He coached three years at Texas Tech and then served as a scout for BLESTO for eight years before joining the Bears' staff.

Rod Graves, youthful and exceptionally bright, holds down a scouting assignment and has recently been promoted to assistant director of player personnel. Based in Atlanta, Graves covers the East and Southeast. He was the assistant director of player personnel for the Philadelphia Stars in the defunct USFL before signing on with the Bears in 1984.

7

Don King, who is set to retire after the 1991 draft is concluded, covers the West Coast and the Southwest, excluding Texas. He has been on the Bears' scouting staff for seven seasons. Before that he spent eleven years as a regional scout for BLESTO, and served as head coach of the University of Hawaii back in 1967.

Charlie Mackey, another onetime BLESTO scout, covers the upper Midwest and Rocky Mountain states. He was formerly an assistant coach at the University of Missouri, and a longtime scout for the Dallas Cowboys under Gil Brandt (1971–88) before joining the Bears.

Ken Geiger, also a BLESTO alumnus, assists in college scouting and handles the scouting of all Bear NFL opponents. He has the additional duties of coordinating tryouts, monitoring NFL transactions, and overseeing the rookie development camp, held each year before training camp. He coached at the Universities of Illinois and Michigan before taking up scouting for the pros.

Jeff Shiver covers the Midwest, a crucial area for the Bears because traditionally they have culled many players from this region. Shiver, too, worked for BLESTO, and before that was an assistant football coach at Purdue and the University of Mississippi.

Head coach Mike Ditka is not expected until later. As far as he is concerned, all the work has been done. All the hours of scouting, film-watching, studying, discussing, and grading have given the Bears a carefully calculated wish-list. The positions they most want to fill have been determined, the players they want to fill them with top the various lists on the wall. Now all they have to do is wait and see which of these players are around when the Bears' first pick comes up, which in 1991 is number 22.

With twenty-one selections going before them, there is some suspense as to whether the more coveted names on the wish-list will still be available when the Bears get to choose, but the general mood is one of confidence that at least one of them will be there for the harvesting.

* * *

Still, one never knows in the draft. The late Paul Brown, legendary coach of the Cleveland Browns (1946–49 in the AAFC, 1950–62 in the NFL) and an enshrinee in the Pro Football Hall of Fame, can vouch for that.

The Browns' great quarterback Otto Graham had retired following the 1955 season after leading Cleveland to four AAFC titles and six consecutive NFL championship games (three of which they won). Without Graham and with injuries hampering his heir, George Ratterman, the Browns had posted their first losing season ever in 1956 (5–7–0). So coach Brown definitely wanted to take a quarterback in the first round of the 1957 draft, one which was especially rich in quarterbacking talent.

Brown had his eye on one of three outstanding prospects: Heisman Trophy winner Paul Hornung of Notre Dame, Stanford's John Brodie, and Len Dawson of Purdue.

The Green Bay Packers had won the Bonus pick that year. The Bonus was something added to the draft in 1947. Each team would draw for the Bonus; the one drawing it would get the first selection in the draft, regardless of where the team ended up in the previous season's standings, in addition to its regular first-round pick. The Bonus was dropped after the 1958 season.

In 1957, after the Bonus pick, the Los Angeles Rams and the San Francisco 49ers had the next two choices in the draft. The Browns, the Baltimore Colts, and the Pittsburgh Steelers were tied for the next pick, all having ended the season with the same dismal records. The Browns lost two consecutive coin tosses, and therefore ended up with the sixth selection in the draft.

Paul Brown had high hopes that one of the three quarterbacks would still be around when his turn came. After all, in the history of the draft, there had never been three quarterbacks selected in the first six choices. Then he sat back and watched in quiet desperation as the Packers took Hornung, the 49ers Brodie, and the Steelers Dawson.

9

An astounded Brown and his colleagues scrambled. They had not imagined a scenario without at least one of the three quarterbacks waiting in the wings for them. After some haggling, and more than a little discussion about two other quarterbacks—still out there were Sonny Jurgensen of Duke and Milt Plum of Penn State—Brown decided that neither warranted first-round selection (Jurgensen went in the fourth round to the Philadelphia Eagles and Plum was picked up by the Browns in the second round). So a dejected Brown had to change his plans. As he later explained, "I decided to settle for a running back instead, so I took this kid from Syracuse, Jim Brown."

In 1991, the Bears do not want a quarterback—not in the first round, anyway. They are happy with Jim Harbaugh, who has firmly established himself as the starter, and they also have Peter Tom Willis, who they took in the third round the year before. And they are not looking for a running back, not with Neal Anderson and Brad Muster entrenched in the backfield and some proven backups for them on the roster, all of whom are healthy.

The Bears, everyone speculates, are in the marketplace for an offensive lineman, because they do not have a starter there under the age of thirty and most are hobbled with one injury or another. The Bears are also looking for a defensive tackle after one of their all-time greats, Dan Hampton, retired in 1990 and Fred Washington, their second-round draft choice that year, was killed in an automobile accident. And they have some interest in a linebacker, one who could be tutored under perennial Pro Bowler Mike Singletary, who plans to retire in a season or two. So that is where most of the talk is directed this Sunday morning.

But they are not just talking about which offensive lineman or defensive lineman or linebacker they will take in the first round. Filling the biggest need is not the overriding criterion. As Bill Tobin explains, "In the broadest sense, we take the best athlete available, but if a need enters in and the athletes are pretty similar, then we'll go to the need factor. But if one player, for example, has a significantly higher Bear grade than a player at which we have a bigger need, then the player personnel department [Bill Tobin] will fight for the higher-graded player.''

Michael McCaskey, who has *the* final say on whom the Bears select, explains further, ''It is simply just not a hard-and-fast rule. It depends on how large the gap in grading is, how pressing the need is, our short-term needs, and our long-term needs. There are many variables which have to be taken into consideration. We do that, and almost always there is a consensus between myself, Bill Tobin, and Mike Ditka as to the player we will select.''

The other topic of conversation around the war room this morning is the fact that Raghib ''Rocket'' Ismail, the speedster from Notre Dame who has come out as a junior and is the player everyone in the league figured to be the first pick in the 1991 draft, announced the night before that he has decided to shun the NFL in favor of the Canadian Football League. The reason: Bruce McNall, owner of the Toronto Argonauts, has made him an offer, as they say, that he cannot refuse—a four-year, personal-services contract for an average salary of $3.5 million, plus incentive clauses and bonuses that could increase the value of the agreement to more than $20 million. He will actually receive $14 million for playing football and $4.2 million in guaranteed endorsements. And those are in U.S. dollars, not Canadian.

Bear scout Jim Parmer shrugs and mentions that the most he ever made playing for the Eagles in the late 1940s and early '50s was $5,000 a season. The price of prime has surely soared.

The Rocket is the reason the Dallas Cowboys traded up to get the first selection, which had belonged to the New England Patriots. The Rocket, by far, garnered the most publicity of all draftees in the weeks preceding the draft, and Cowboy owner Jerry Jones, who keeps no fishhooks in his pocket when it comes to snagging a superstar—witness the extravagant multimillion-dollar contract he gave quarterback Troy Aikman two years earlier—wanted the alluring name of Raghib Ismail on his roster. But even Jones could not handle the price tag demanded for the Rocket to stay in the United States and play in the NFL: a guaranteed four-year contract for $16 million and an incentive package worth another $4 million. As Jones explained, "We made good-faith negotiations with the Rocket, but his numbers were totally out of our range." So the Rocket became the first potential number one pick since linebacker Tom Cousineau in 1979 to sign with the Canadian Football League.

The Bears didn't care. They had been contacted a month earlier by the New England Patriots about trading up for the number one pick—the Pats wanted volume, not just one potential superstar. But the Bears were not interested in Rocket and his astronomical price tag. As Mike Ditka wryly observed, "That's an awful lot for a special-teams player, a kick returner." He was referring to the fact that while the Bears and a lot of other teams' scouting reports conceded the Rocket's speed and his great moves, they also noted that as a wide receiver he had problems catching the football.

Rocket's expatriation throws off the Bears' mock draft. They had him picked to go number one no matter who came up with the first choice. But *mock* drafts are just that—exercises in guessing what the other teams want or will take depending on the availabilities that are there when their selection comes up. Michael McCaskey refers to mock drafts as nothing more than "training exercises to get the thinking muscles in tone for draft day." The only real effect Rocket's emigration to Canada has on the Bears is that with Rocket's name erased from the list of potential first-round draftees, it increases the chances by one that someone the Bears *do* want won't be there when the first round gets down to number 22.

It is now noon in New York, 11 A.M. in Dallas. The only team that knows for sure which player it is going to get in the first round is the Cowboys. In the other twenty-seven war rooms, the clubs' cadres wait, ready to alter their wish-lists or reassess their priorities.

A few minutes later NFL commissioner Paul Tagliabue steps to the podium, looks at the small sheet of paper in his hand, and announces, "The Dallas Cowboys select defensive tackle Russell Maryland of Miami." And the 1991 NFL draft is off and running.

2

GETTING THERE

The road to the 1991 NFL draft actually began on the roads that lead from UCLA to USC, Alabama to Auburn, Michigan to Ohio State, TCU to Texas A & M, and hundreds of other well-traveled ways. And it began three years earlier, when the scouts of all twenty-eight teams set out on their journeys from school to school, when the current crop of seniors were sophomores who were about to start their college football careers.

Shortly after each year's draft, the scouts head for spring practices at the colleges, the latest combine reports and ratings in hand, to continue the preparation for next year's draft. In the case of the Chicago Bears, it is the BLESTO combine findings that their scouts tote along with them.

BLESTO is an acronym for Bears-Lions-Eagles-Steelers Talent Organization. These were the only four teams subscribing to it in 1964 (it had been known as LESTO until the Bears joined that year). Today there are seven other teams that subscribe to BLESTO besides the Bears, Lions, and Steelers, (the Eagles no longer do)—the Dallas Cowboys, Minnesota Vikings, Miami Dolphins, Washington Redskins, New York Giants, Buffalo Bills, and Indianapolis Colts—which would make adding their first initials to the acronym a little awkward, so it remains in name the same as it was almost three decades ago.

Essentially, BLESTO gathers vital information on four to five thousand college football players. The BLESTO scouts look at them first in spring practice of their junior year and then throughout their senior year. Only about a thousand of them are considered prospects, and only 336 will be selected in the draft's twelve rounds.

The combine is headed by Jack Butler, who directs the entire operation from BLESTO's home office in Pittsburgh, as he has been doing since its inception in 1963. It has eight area scouts, two regional scouts, and one national scout. As a result, each prospect is studied by four scouting specialists.

The information collected is evaluated and then a grade for each player is determined. The information includes things like height and weight, speed in the 40-yard sprint, known injuries, statistics; these are the basics. There is also grading for such things as strength, attitude, aggressiveness, character, intelligence, quickness, and lateral movement. And, of course, each player is graded on his position skills.

When all the measurements and grades are evaluated, the player is given an overall grade within a range of 0.0 to 4.1. The highest ranking, 0.0, is a perfect grade, but no one is perfect. The highest grade ever given, according to Jack Butler, was 0.4, earned by O. J. Simpson when he was at Southern Cal in 1968. Only a few check in at under 1.0, among them Tony Dorsett at Pittsburgh in 1976, John Elway at Stanford in 1982, and Troy Aikman at UCLA in 1988.

Within the BLESTO grading system, anything under 1.0 is considered a franchise-maker, a player who will become an NFL superstar. A grading between 1.0 and 1.5 indicates the player may very well be a starter his rookie year. Between 2.0 and 2.5, the player has a good shot at making one of the NFL teams. Up to 3.0 a player is considered a possible. Above that it is highly unlikely a player will make the wall in an NFL war room, unless there is some information or grading from a team's own scouts that puts BLESTO's evaluation in question. A player's grade can easily change from the time the first BLESTO scout takes a look at him to the final grade that is given him after his senior-year season is over. The final grade is put on a player by Jack Butler after meeting with the scouts once the college season has ended.

BLESTO's information and grading is then made available to all teams that subscribe to the combine; it is simply a common resource. Each ball club uses it in its own way, combining the information and gradings with those of its own scouts and the evaluations made by its own player personnel director, and, in some instances, its coaching staff or even its general manager or club president. It costs a team in the 1990s about $120,000 a year to subscribe to BLESTO's services.

The whole idea of draft combines goes back to the early 1960s. It was the time of the Great War—not World War I, but the one the NFL waged with the fledgling American Football League. Franchise revenues, especially with the financial competition for talent as a result of the Great War, were not very impressive.

Serious scouting of college talent was essential by this time, but it was also costly. Not only were there all the major colleges with top-flight talent, ranging from Syracuse to UCLA, Florida to the U. of Washington, and all those in between, but there also were the minor colleges, where gemstones could be discovered— like Andy Robustelli, whom the Rams found at Arnold College, which had an enrollment of 350 and does not even exist anymore; or Deacon Jones, another Ram discovery, found down at Mississippi Vocational; or Tony Canadeo of Gonzaga University in Spokane, Washington, whom coach Curly Lambeau of the Packers heard about from a friend. All of them were unique discoveries who made it to the Pro Football Hall of Fame.

So to make it economically feasible to ferret out the best of the college talent, teams took to creating combines—joint ventures in scouting. Over the years there have been a number of them;

16

S- 3811 DEFENSE-BLESTO INC. SENIOR ABILITY REPORT

Scout's Name _____

Previous Grade _____

Date [ ][ ][ ][ ][ ][ ] School No. [ ][ ][ ][ ] Jersey No. [ ][ ] Sc'ts. No. [ ][ ][ ] Sc'ts. Rate [ ][ ][ ]

SCHOOL _____ STATE _____

Player [ ]

NAME _____ FIRST _____

Pro Pos. [ ] Ht. [ ][ ] Est. Meas. ☐ Wt. [ ][ ] Est. ☐ Spring ☐ Wgd. ☐ Fall ☐ Time [ ][ ] Est ☐ | F Pads | Grass | Rel Prac | Conditions
Blesto ☐ | P Pads | Astro | Alt Prac | Wet | Wind | Blks.

College Pos. [ ][ ] Wt. Pot. [ ][ ][ ] Body-Leg Structure [ ][ ] Dist [ ][ ] Scout ☐ | Shorts | Track | Spring | Dry | Ideal | In Dst.

EEO [ ][ ] Marital Status [ ] Children [ ] Right ☐ Left ☐ Hand ☐ Foot ☐ Birth Date [ ][ ][ ][ ][ ][ ]

Report Based On: Personal Observation [ ] Coaches Etc. [ ] Games [ ] Game Film [ ] _____

0 GENERAL	5 DEFENSIVE BACK	DS	DW	6 DEFENSIVE LINEMAN	DT	DE	7 LINEBACKER	MB	LB	8 RETURN SPECIALIST
Athletic Ability	Accell-Burst			Accell-Burst			Tackling			Judgement
Strength & Explosion	Man Cover			Explosion Off Ball			Stay On Feet			Hands
Playing Speed/Accell.	Quick Feet			In Line Play			In Line Play			Quickness
Quickness/Body Control	Turn Ability			Strength At Point			Shed-Use Hands			Elusiveness
Durability	Quickness Off Turn			Shed-Use Hands			Reaction			Courage
Ability To Learn F.B.	Zone Cover			Reaction			Strength At Point			9 KICKING SPECIALIST
Instinctive Ability	Vision			Stay On Feet			Range			Leg Strength
Citizenship	F.B. Reactions			Lat. Quickness			Lat. Quickness			Consistency
Competitive./Toughness	Hands			Change Direction			Change Direction			Quickness
Work Habits	Jumping			Pursuit			Pass Cover			Accuracy
Consistency	Run Support			Pass Rush			Catching			Poise
Production	Tackling			Tackling			Blitzing			Style C ☐ Hang Time . / S ☐ Aver. Dist. .

Home Address [ ]

City [ ][ ][ ][ ][ ][ ][ ][ ][ ][ ][ ][ ][ ][ ][ ][ ][ ][ ][ ] State [ ][ ][ ] Zip Code [ ][ ][ ][ ][ ] Area Code [ ][ ][ ] Phone [ ][ ][ ][ ][ ][ ][ ][ ]

PRO PHYS. POTENTIAL [ ]   COLLEGE PERFORMANCE [ ]   PROJ. PRO PERFORMANCE [ ]

Injury [ ]   TEST SCORE [ ][ ] OF _____ TIMES TAKEN _____

COMMENTS

STRENGTH: _____

SLIGHTLY ABOVE AVER.: _____

WEAKNESS: _____

PROJ. PRO PERFORMANCE: _____

Line-Up Position & Jersey Number	Special Team Player:	Type of Runner			Yr. Entered College	Draft Round
○ ○○ X ○○○ ○	Yes [ ] No [ ]	Fluid ☐ Loose ☐ Stiff ☐ Compact ☐ Labors ☐ Long Stride ☐	Glasses ☐ Contacts ☐		Red _____ Shirted _____ GPA _____ Transfer _____	

17

S- 4203 OFFENSE-BLESTO INC. SENIOR ABILITY REPORT

Scout's Name _____

Previous Grade _____

Date [ ][ ][ ][ ]   School No. [ ][ ][ ]   Jersey No. [ ][ ]   Sc'ts. No. [ ][ ][ ]   Sc'ts. Rate [ ][ ]

SCHOOL   STATE

Player [ ][ ][ ][ ][ ][ ][ ][ ][ ][ ][ ][ ][ ][ ][ ]   [ ][ ][ ][ ][ ][ ][ ][ ][ ][ ]

NAME   FIRST

Pro Pos. [ ][ ]   Ht. [ ][ ] . [ ]   Est. Meas. ☐ Wt. [ ][ ]   Est. Wgd. ☐   Spring ☐ Fall ☐   Time [ ][ ]   Est. [ ]   F Pads [ ] Grass [ ] Bef Prac [ ]   Conditions

College Pos. [ ][ ]   Wt. Pot. [ ][ ]   Body-Leg Structure [ ][ ]   Dist [ ]   Blesto [ ] P Pads [ ] Astro [ ] Aft Prac [ ]   Wet [ ] Wind [ ] Bks [ ]

EEO [ ][ ]   Marital Status [ ]   Children [ ]   Right ☐ Left ☐   Hand ☐ Foot ☐   Birth Date [ ][ ][ ][ ][ ]

Scout [ ] Shorts [ ] Track [ ]   Spring [ ] Dry [ ] Ideal [ ] In Drs [ ]

Report Based On: Personal Observation ☐   Coaches Etc. ☐   Games ☐   Game Film ☐ _____

0 GENERAL	1 OFFENSIVE BACK	HB	FB	2 OFFENSIVE LINEMAN	C OG	OT	3 OFFENSIVE RECEIVER	WR	TE	4 QUARTERBACK
Athletic Ability	Quick Start			In Line Block			Acceleration			Arm Strength
Strength & Explosion	Accell-Burst			Block On Move			Quickness			Quick Release
Playing Speed/Accell	Outside Run			Pop Explosion			Hands			Accuracy
Quickness/Body Control	Elusiveness			Stays On Feet			Ball Concentration			Field Vision
Durability	Balance			Balance			Competitive Rec.			Touch
Ability To Learn F.B.	Change Direction			Pulling			Tough Catch			Short Pass
Instinctive Ability	Inside Run			Pass Block Pot.			Separation			Deep Pass
Citizenship	Run Strength			Use of Hands			Adjust To Ball			Set Up Quick
Competitive/Toughness	Hands-Rec.			Lateral Movement			Jumping			Movement In Pocket
Work Habits	Pass Routes			Quick Feet			Run After Catch			Scramble
Consistency	Blocking			Leg Strength			Fumbler			Courage
Production	Non Fumble			Long Snap			Blocking			Leadership

Home Address [ ]

City [ ][ ][ ][ ][ ][ ][ ][ ][ ][ ][ ][ ]   State [ ][ ]   Zip Code [ ][ ][ ][ ][ ]   Area Code [ ][ ][ ]   Phone [ ][ ][ ][ ][ ][ ][ ]

PRO PHYS. POTENTIAL [ ]   COLLEGE PERFORMANCE [ ]   PROJ. PRO PERFORMANCE [ ]

Injury [ ]   TEST SCORE [ ][ ] OF _____ TIMES TAKEN _____

COMMENTS

STRENGTH: _____

_____

SLIGHTLY ABOVE AVER: _____

_____

WEAKNESS: _____

_____

PROJ. PRO PERFORMANCE: _____

_____

Line-Up Position & Jersey Number	Special Team Player:	Type of Runner			Yr. Entered	Draft
O O O X O O O O	Yes ☐ No ☐	Fluid ☐ Stiff ☐ Labors ☐	Loose ☐ Compact ☐ Long Stride ☐	Glasses ☐ Contacts ☐	College ___ Red Shirted ___ GPA ___ Transfer ___	Round

besides BLESTO, the National, Galaxy, Troika, CEPO, and Quadro. Only BLESTO and National have survived into the 1990s. Only four teams today do not belong to either BLESTO or National: the Los Angeles Raiders, San Francisco 49ers, Denver Broncos, and Tampa Bay Buccaneers.

Having these combine ratings does not really change the scouts' job. They still visit the schools, talk to the coaches and trainers, watch game films, snoop around for some inside information, come up with their own ratings or personal feelings about a player, and so forth. But the combine scouting and grading does give them a start, a base from which to launch their own investigations.

BLESTO, to the Bears and its other subscribers, is essentially a data base of facts; it does not contain the kind of personal information that a seasoned scout can pick up with his own eye or ear or gut feeling, which might very much influence a team's decision on the day of the draft. The players may be looked on as meat—graded, as a grisly NFL scout put it, "prime, choice, economy, or dog food"—but football is an emotional game played by human beings with varying senses of dedication, different degrees of heart, diverse personalities. These are things that the scout will be looking for to add to the potential pro's biography.

It is the team scout who ordinarily comes up with the sleeper, the player overlooked or underrated by the combines and the other teams. It was back in 1979 that Jim Parmer, who in his twenty-six-year scouting career has looked at players in every state of the union except Alaska and Maine, sat down with Jim Finks, then the Bears' general manager and chief operating officer, for a little "chat session."

Parmer, a member of the old school of scouts who chats with everybody at the schools he visits, from the head football coach to the athletic department secretary, relies a lot on instinct. With his slow Texas drawl—he lives in Abilene, Texas, and used to do a little drinking down in those environs with that immortal carouser and Hall of Fame quarterback, the late Bobby Layne—he expresses his philosophy: "Sometimes you just have a feel for a kid; something sends you a message."

It did in 1979. BLESTO did not have a very high rating on a defensive tackle from Arkansas by the name of Dan Hampton. Hampton was hardly a sleeper, but there were question marks in the combine gradings. He had the size (6'5", 270 pounds) and credentials (All-America his senior year) but his speed was questionable. BLESTO had clocked him at 5:2 in the 40-yard dash, not very impressive. And there was some question about his durability—he had had a bad accident as a youth, breaking both legs in a fall from a tree.

The Bears were in the market for defensive linemen that year and they had the fourth pick in the draft. There was a lot of skepticism around the front office and in the coaching enclave, however, about taking Hampton in the first round, given his low grading from BLESTO. But Parmer had seen him play for three years on his rounds, one stop of which included Fayetteville, Arkansas, and he had "a strong feel for the kid."

So, in his chat session with Finks, he lobbied strongly for Hampton. Finks told Parmer to go back down to Arkansas and personally grade him again, get some more information, see if he still had the feel. Parmer clocked Hampton at 4:8 in the 40 and learned that when BLESTO had timed him earlier Hampton had been hampered with a slightly pulled muscle. This is an example of why old-line scouts subscribe to the Mark Twain axiom "There are three types of lies: lies, damn lies, and statistics."

Parmer came back to Chicago with the feel not only intact but enhanced. He convinced Jim Finks, Bill Tobin, and then-head coach Neill Armstrong, and the Bears took Hampton with the fourth pick in the first round of the 1979 draft. The rest is history: Dan Hampton became a starter his rookie year, played twelve years for the Bears, went to numerous Pro Bowls, and was named to the All-NFL team of the 1980s by the Pro Football Hall of Fame Board of Selectors.

A true sleeper found by Parmer was a fullback from the less-than-nationally-known Louisiana Tech, Roland Harper. Parmer suggested to Finks, "If this kid's around in the last round, take him." He was, and the Bears took him in the seventeenth round, the 420th selection of the 1975 draft (the NFL draft was not reduced to twelve rounds until 1977). Harper, in his eight-year Bear career, went on to become the fifth most productive rusher in the team's seventy-year-plus history (3,044 yards), and provided hundreds of key blocks for the NFL's all-time leading rusher, Walter Payton.

Probably the best example of scouting serendipity, however, was provided by the Dallas Cowboys under Gil Brandt. He and his scouts unearthed an abundance of Pro Bowl–quality players from some very unlikely sources, including defensive tackle Jethro Pugh, Elizabeth City State College (North Carolina); safety Cliff Harris, Ouachita Baptist College (Arkansas); tackle Rayfield Wright, Fort Valley State (Georgia); tight end Pettis Norman, Johnson C. Smith University (North Carolina); linebacker Thomas "Hollywood" Henderson, Langston (Oklahoma); and guard Herbert Scott, Virginia Union (Virginia), to name but a few. While he ran the player-personnel aspect of the Dallas Cowboys, Brandt knew no bounds and his scouting tentacles reached everywhere. In 1962, he signed as a free agent Cornell Green of Utah State, who was not a college football player but instead an All-American basketball player. Brandt then let Tom Landry turn Green into a four-time All-Pro and five-time Pro Bowl cornerback.

Brandt took Bob Hayes, the world record holder in the 100-yard dash and destined to win the Olympic gold medal in the 100-meter dash (1964), in the seventh round of the 1963 draft. Although Hayes was not recognized for having any particularly notable football skills, Brandt saw him as a game-breaking wide receiver. Hayes went on to become a two-time All-Pro and one of the Cowboys' all-time leading pass catchers.

That same year Brandt drafted Navy quarterback Roger Staubach in the tenth round, even though he knew Staubach had a four-year military commitment facing him. Brandt even recruited kicker Toni Fritsch from Vienna, Austria, in 1971.

Brandt relied a lot on the use of the computer in running his drafting operation down in Dallas. As he explains: "We used the computer as a method of taking the human faults out of the evaluation of football players. We found out that if you put good final information into the computer, you're going to get a very good reading out of the computer. Whereas sometimes people—individuals—let their feelings take a better part of their judgment, the computer doesn't.

"Sometimes you'll go to a school, and if a player is very polite to you and pleads he always wanted to play with the Cowboys, that sticks out in your mind. Whereas you go to another school and another player's answer is, All I want to do is play where the most money is. When you make a final decision based on those kinds of statements, it's easy to go with the one who has told you he loves the Cowboys and always wanted to play in Dallas. But that is not a very good reason for picking a player. The computer doesn't judge that way."

There is no question that Gil Brandt was exceptional at what he accomplished in stocking the Cowboys in the 1960s, '70s, and '80s. But there is some question as to what the computer really had to do with it. As Bill Tobin notes: "The teams that try to computerize it [scouting/grading] are missing the boat. There are just too many factors. Many people got misled because of the mystique of the Cowboys in those years and what they were doing with the computer. But I don't think it was the computer. What they did do was a great job in trading around to move up in various drafts."

That the Cowboys and Brandt indeed did do. Some of the

outstanding players they obtained by trading up in the draft were defensive tackle Bob Lilly, a number one from Cleveland in 1961; safety Charlie Waters, number three from Houston through Cleveland in 1970; defensive end Harvey Martin, number three from Houston through New Orleans in 1973; defensive end Ed "Too Tall" Jones, number one, and quarterback/punter Danny White, number three, both from Houston in 1974; defensive tackle Randy White, number one from the Giants in 1975; running back Tony Dorsett, number one from Seattle, and wide receiver Tony Hill, number three from Philadelphia, both in 1977; and running back Herschel Walker, number five from Houston in 1985. And there were plenty of others acquired that way who inscribed their names in Dallas Cowboy lore.

"So much of scouting is feel," Tobin explains. "It's human grading human. Granted there are going to be mistakes, but there are so many other factors that a computer can't interpret or evaluate. That's why the scouts have to have their own built-in memory bank. They have to be able to compare, to bring up insights from the past, whether it is about the same player he saw two years ago and had a certain feeling for or whether it was something special he sees in a player that reminds him of what he saw once, say, in a Joe Namath or a Lawrence Taylor. There are subjective things as well as objective things that have to be taken into consideration, which is what we do in arriving at a final Bear grade on a prospect. Memory bank!"

Michael McCaskey obviously agrees with Tobin's philosophy. He says: "The Bears are not a computerized scouting/rating system. We rely on the judgments and instincts of an experienced staff on top of the raw data. We look to their [the scouts'] assessments, and we want them to be strong enough to stick to their guns, hold to their convictions." And he adds as an aside: "The Cowboys may not have even been the first team to use the computer, but they were the first one to brag about it."

3

THE
SCOUTING
GAME

An NFL scout's life is hardly a glamorous one. It is, in fact, an arduous one: constant travel; long days watching films and talking to someone, anyone, who can give you that little extra bit of information; and the paperwork; and the meals on the road; and the hours in the evening in the motel room making notes and reports. And the next morning, as Willie Nelson might sing, "On the road again . . ."

It can, of course, be a gratifying life if, say, after sixteen rounds of the draft have gone by, you recommend to your team that they take this otherwise unheralded quarterback from Alabama named Bart Starr, as one Green Bay Packer scout did in 1956.

Or perhaps you suggest that the team take a look at this free agent wide receiver, as a Dallas Cowboy scout did in 1973, after every team in the NFL had bypassed him in the draft. Tom Landry took the advice, liked what he saw, and the Cowboys signed Drew Pearson from the University of Tulsa. Without that scout's suggestion, pro football fans would have been deprived of the famous Hail Mary pass (Roger Staubach to Pearson, a 50-yarder for a touchdown with twenty-four seconds to go in the 1975 playoff game that gave the Cowboys a 17–14 upset victory over the Minnesota Vikings and enabled them to go to Super Bowl X). And Dallas fans would not have seen Drew Pearson, over the next eight years, catch the most passes (378) in team history.

On the other hand, it can be frustrating. In 1979, the Green Bay Packers were drafting ahead of the San Francisco 49ers. The scouts, to a man, lobbied for drafting Notre Dame quarterback Joe Montana. As the head coach, Bart Starr overruled them, even in the third round of the draft, opting instead to draft running backs Eddie Lee Ivery and Steve Atkins and defensive tackle Charles Johnson. The 49ers listened to their scouts that year.

A typical day in the life of an NFL scout is, as Don King, who until his retirement in 1991 covered the West for the Bears, noted, "very long." King, who was based out of his home in Sun Lakes, Arizona, spent his days in much the same way as the current staff scouts of the Bears do.

"I usually got up around four or five in the morning, went out and got in the car to drive to a particular school. I set it up so I would arrive there about nine. I'd visit the trainer to get an update on the player's injury situation, the position coach to check on the kid's work habits, things like that. I would watch films for most of the day; I'd try to eventually watch five games on each player we had a high rating on or were especially interested in. At three o'clock, I'd go out and watch practice. There's a lot you can pick up watching a kid when he's working out at practice. About six-thirty I'd get a bite to eat and then go back to the motel room. The reports have to be done the same day, while they're still fresh in your mind. I ordinarily tape-recorded the reports and then typed them up and sent them off to Bill Tobin back at Halas Hall. The next morning I would head on to another school."

Every day, of course, is not exactly the same. Sometimes a scout will fly to a school; sometimes he will go just to investigate a single player; sometimes he will be cross-checking the work of another scout.

Today, scouting is a full-time, year-round job. A typical year begins with D-Day in April. Once D-Day is over, the scouts stay around team headquarters to assess who *wasn't* drafted—to search for worthy free agents. After all, more than a few acknowledged greats in the game of pro football were overlooked in various drafts and picked up as free agents, such stalwarts as defensive backs Dick "Night Train" Lane, who had played at Scottsbluff Junior College in Nebraska and was grabbed by the Los Angeles Rams, and Emlen Tunnell of Toledo, signed by the New York Giants; defensive tackle Art Donovan from Boston College, obtained by the Baltimore Colts; and running back Joe Perry, who never went to a four-year college but was spotted by a scout for the San Francisco 49ers while he was playing football for a military service team. All eventually got themselves a plaque in the Pro Football Hall of Fame.

In the Bear den, once the draft has been concluded, Bill Tobin sits down with the scouts, reviews the draft, talks about team needs, discusses who is still left around. Now is a time for the scouts to shine, to lobby for the players who they have studied and who they see as sleepers.

After going over the free-agency pool and making recommendations, the scouts stay around for the team's mini-camp, which in the 1990s is held shortly after the draft, sit in on coaches' meetings, and observe workouts.

In May, it is on the road again to college spring practices and the daily routine of talking to the college team staffs, watching films, and writing or updating reports. The month of June and perhaps the first two weeks in July, they are off—"off" in the sense that they are not traveling. They are at home, but it is a time of massive paperwork, organizing all the data they have collected and have received from BLESTO, and finalizing their personal observations or gut feelings. It is not a time of rest and relaxation.

In mid-July they come to training camp, look at the crop of draftees, and meet with the coaches. As the teams move into their preseason games, they pare their rosters, and the scouts study those players who have been released by other teams in the hope of finding someone their team might be interested in.

A shining example of what might be out there: Johnny Unitas was cut by the Pittsburgh Steelers in 1955 and picked up as a free agent by the Baltimore Colts. Jim Finks remembers when the Bears decided to take a chance on safety Gary Fencik, released by the Miami Dolphins in 1976; Fencik became a mainstay in their defensive backfield for twelve seasons and still holds the all-time club record for pass interceptions (38).

After the free-agency pool is analyzed, it's time to visit the colleges again. From mid-August to mid-November, it is a six-day week: Monday through Friday in athletic departments, locker rooms, film rooms, and at practices; Saturday at the game, and sometimes parts of two games if the timing and distance allow for it. Jim Parmer remembers taking in two games on a Saturday on quite a few occasions—maybe a Texas Christian game in Fort Worth and a later-starting Southern Methodist game over in Dallas. Or maybe the first half of a Tulane game in New Orleans and the second half of a Louisiana State game in Baton Rouge.

The scouts are not the only ones hitting the road for the Bears. Bill Tobin is, too. He is out there visiting every major school in the country to make his own personal reports and gradings. He, in effect, is doing the same thing his scouts are: talking to position coaches, watching films, getting medical updates from trainers . . .

Meanwhile the scouts' reports are flowing into Halas Hall, into

Tobin's office there. They go directly to his secretary, who duly logs them in. But Tobin does not want to see or hear about them. "I want the slate clean when I go to see a player," Tobin explains. "I don't want to be influenced by another opinion before I see the player for myself. The only things I want to be alerted to that would come from one of the scout's reports would be if a guy is injured or not playing for one reason or another or is being red-shirted so I don't bother going to that school to see him. If something like that comes in, my secretary will flag it for me and let me know." It is not until after the bowl games and college postseason all-star games that he sits down to study the scouts' reports.

When the college season ends in mid-November, the scouts spend the next month or so cross-checking the information and gradings that each other have come up with. The cross-checks are then submitted to Bill Tobin.

After that there are the numerous bowl games and, most importantly, the all-star games: Senior Bowl, East–West, Blue–Gray, and the Hula Bowl. At least two scouts go to each all-star game and to the practice sessions preceding them.

February is the month of the NFL scouting combine, an official league function during which the four hundred or so top prospects are brought to one location, where they are scrutinized by NFL coaches, player personnel directors, scouts, trainers, team doctors, and often owners.

In March, most of the NCAA Division 1-A schools and many of the smaller ones hold a Pro Day, set aside for the various team and combine scouts, bearing stopwatches and clipboards, to weigh, test, and update medical profiles of potential draftees.

About three weeks before D-Day, the scouts come to team headquarters and begin to help organize the war room. In the case of the Chicago Bears, it takes approximately one hundred hours to put their wall lists in order.

And then there is D-Day—the day they have been working toward for the previous three years.

28

4

IT WASN'T ALWAYS THIS WAY

Scouting, needless to say, has not always been the sophisticated, technological operation it is in the 1990s. In fact, in earlier times there were no full-time scouts. The coaches and owners of teams relied on things like word of mouth—tips from former players, or from a friendly college coach, or perhaps from a friend who was impressed with what he saw at a college game and passed it along.

Another way to gather information about prospects was to read articles in magazines and accounts of games in newspapers and in almanacs like *Street & Smith's Yearbook*. That was the method employed by Wellington Mara, who is today 50 percent owner of the New York Giants, the team his father, Tim Mara, founded in 1925.

Wellington, at age sixteen, took on the job that in the 1990s would be called director of player personnel. He immersed himself in as many writings about college football as he could get his hands on, developed lists of players at each position, and then presented them to his father and to longtime (1926–53) Giant coach Steve Owen.

It was through this research that he found out about Tuffy Leemans. It was autumn 1935, and Wellington was then a nineteen-year-old student at Fordham University in New York. He went to his father and told him he had read in a Washington, D.C., newspaper about this promising running back who played for George Washington University. Wellington said he wanted to go there and see for himself and perhaps talk to Leemans. Tim Mara agreed.

When Wellington approached Leemans down in Washington, the running back mistook him for a kid wanting an autograph. After Wellington straightened out this minor embarrassment, he talked to Leemans about joining the Giants. Leemans was interested. The Giants drafted him in the second round of the first NFL draft, and Leemans went on to become one of the finest running backs in Giant history and a member of the Pro Football Hall of Fame.

That was the way it was done in the 1930s.

And that was an improvement, because by 1936 at least the colleges were to some degree cooperating with the pros—which had not been the case in the earliest years of the NFL.

Years before the draft was formalized to regulate the rostering of college-trained players in the NFL, the league had tried to coexist with the colleges. The team owners knew that the colleges were their Triple A, Double A, and Class A minor leagues all rolled into one.

Those who controlled the game at the college level, however, hardly shared such sentiments of coexistence. The venerable Amos Alonzo Stagg, known as the "Grand Old Man" of the college game, summed up his feelings with this statement: "For years, the colleges have been waging a bitter warfare against the insidious forces of the gambling public and alumni and against overzealous and short-sighted friends, inside and out, and also not infrequently against crooked coaches and managers, who have been anxious to win at any cost. . . . And now comes along another serious menace, possibly greater than all others, *viz.* Sunday professional football.''

The menacing pros had, however, incorporated into their four-tenet Code of Ethics, authored by NFL President Joe Carr himself in the early 1920s, this, the longest and most emphatic of the four precepts:

Tampering with players on College teams shall not be tolerated by this league. The same creates much unfavorable sentiment against professional football and is deplored and discouraged by this league.

Well, maybe it wasn't deplored all that much. It was pretty clear in 1925 that the Chicago Bears had done a little tampering when Red Grange, already a football legend, slipped out of his University of Illinois uniform one Saturday in late November and donned a Bears one the following Thursday to make his pro football debut in a Thanksgiving Day game against the Bears' then crosstown rivals, the Chicago Cardinals.

The matriculation of Grange to the pros and the ensuing two barnstorming tours he made with the Bears in late 1925 and early 1926 put professional football on the proverbial map. The tours took them out east, where they played to about 72,000 fans at the Polo Grounds at a time when the Giants, then in their first year in the NFL, were ordinarily drawing about 10,000 spectators to a game, and not all of them paying customers. The proceeds from the Grange/Bears game, it is said, saved the Giant franchise, the team having been about $40,000 in the red before it.

The games on the two tours played to packed stadiums in other cities on the East Coast and in the Midwest, down in Florida, out in California, and finally up in Seattle. The tours, incidentally, put about $100,000 in the Chicago franchise's otherwise paltry purse and about $250,000 in twenty-one-year-old Red Grange's pocket, thanks to the deal worked out by his agent, C. C. "Cash & Carry" Pyle, the game's first agent and the man who entrepreneured the barnstorming tours.

Grange's entry into the NFL may have been a boon to the Bears and to professional football in general, but it did little to endear the game to the already skeptical college coaches throughout the land. Grange's coach at Illinois, Bob Zuppke, would not even talk to the Galloping Ghost for several years after Grange's jump to the NFL.

Seeing the error of his ways or, perhaps, as some have suggested, seeing to it that nobody else could ever pull off the coup he had, player/coach/owner George Halas of the Bears introduced a new rule at the 1926 league meeting prohibiting any NFL team from acquiring a college player whose class had not yet graduated. It was quickly adopted.

It was also soon violated . . . by George Halas. In need of a running back near the end of the 1930 season, Halas signed Joe Savoldi, who had toted the pigskin earlier that year for Notre Dame. The story, according to Halas:

Savoldi arrived at the Bears' office in Chicago a day or two after the college season ended in mid-November. He explained that he had been unceremoniously ousted from school because he had secretly gotten married, which was against Notre Dame's rules in those days. Now he needed a job and he wanted to play pro football, right away—or so Halas maintained. So Savoldi was signed to a Bear contract.

Halas then issued this statement: "I conclude that Joe Savoldi is no longer a student. After all, he has been removed from the rolls of the university. Because of the extraordinary circumstances surrounding the case we do not feel that we are making any encroachment upon college football, nor does this set any precedent of jeopardizing the amateur standing of any college player, as Savoldi is no longer classed as a college player. So we are happy and proud to announce that Joe Savoldi will appear in uniform as one of our regular players to participate in our big game next Thanksgiving morning against the Cardinals.'' Then Halas added as an aside to the assembled newsmen, ''His coming to us was somewhat of a miracle.''

League president Joe Carr failed to see the miraculousness of it, however, and fined the Bears $1,000 for permitting Savoldi to play in that big game against the Cardinals.

In 1935, Bert Bell, the owner of the Philadelphia Eagles who would later serve as NFL commissioner, came up with a proposal aimed at developing parity in the league. For the most part during those early years, the NFL was dominated by the Chicago Bears, Green Bay Packers, and New York Giants, while the Philadelphia Eagles, Chicago Cardinals, and Pittsburgh Pirates (they would not become the Steelers until 1941) perennially languished at the bottom of the pile.

Bell's brainchild was for the NFL to conduct a formal college draft to enable the weaker teams to obtain the top college talent and in that way make themselves more competitive. NFL teams would draft in the inverse order of their finish the season before; the team with the worst record would get the first draft choice and the team winning the NFL title would get the last. His motivation may have been strengthened by the fact that his Eagles had not had a winning season since they'd entered the NFL in 1933 and, in fact, had turned in the worst record in the league in 1935 (2–9–0).

The other owners agreed, however. If the league was to survive, there had to be more equal competition. After all, it was the heart of the Depression, and if a team did not get paying spectators into its park, it was not going to remain in business very long. Restricting the draft to players who had finished their college eligibility, it was felt, would also mollify the ill feelings many college coaches still had for the pros.

So, on February 8, 1936, the owners of the nine NFL teams

met in the Ritz-Carlton Hotel in Philadelphia. On hand were Bert Bell of the Eagles, George Halas of the Bears, George Preston Marshall of the Redskins (then of Boston), Art Rooney of the Pittsburgh Pirates, Curly Lambeau of the Packers, Bill Bidwill of the Cardinals, Tim Mara of the Giants, George Richards of the Lions, and Dan Topping of the Brooklyn Dodgers.

Each team was allotted one table, and on one wall there was a list of ninety players whose college eligibility was over from which each team would make its choices. There were to be nine rounds. The ninety names were substantially drawn from various All-America and All-Conference teams selected after the 1935 season. There were no scouts in attendance, no gradings, ratings, biographical data, health reports. As they sat at their little tables, the owners were relying solely on what they had read in the newspapers and magazines, or perhaps what they had heard from so-called friends of the family.

The Eagles had the first pick and selected Heisman Trophy winner and All-America halfback Jay Berwanger of the University of Chicago. Then Bert Bell promptly traded Berwanger to the Bears for two-year-veteran tackle Art Buss. The trade was not a wise move on the part of George Halas and the Bears, because Berwanger had no intention of playing professional football and went into business in Chicago instead.

The Bears, however, made two other moves that D-Day that could be defined as wise; they drafted two future Hall of Famers, tackle Joe Stydahar of West Virginia and guard Danny Fortmann from Colgate. There were two other future enshrinees in the Pro Football Hall of Fame that first draft, halfback Tuffy Leemans of the New York Giants and end Wayne Millner of Notre Dame, an eighth-round choice of the Boston Redskins.

Stydahar, a 6'4", 230-pound tackle, was the Bears' first-round choice. The Bears have traditionally been quite successful with their first-round draft choices over the years. Besides Stydahar, they have made seven other first-round selections over the years who would eventually end up in the Hall of Fame in Canton, Ohio: Sid Luckman (Columbia, 1939), Bulldog Turner (Hardin-Simmons, 1940), George McAfee (Duke, 1940), Bobby Layne (Texas, 1948), Mike Ditka (Pittsburgh, 1961), Dick Butkus (Illinois, 1965), and Gale Sayers (Kansas, 1965). And they have two others who are pretty safe bets to end up in the Hall when they become eligible: Walter Payton (Jackson State, 1975) and Dan Hampton (Arkansas, 1979). The Bears, incidentally, are the only team in NFL history to twice draft two future Hall of Famers in the first round in the same year, Turner and McAfee in 1940 and Butkus and Sayers in 1965.

After Berwanger was taken by the Eagles, the Redskins took an All-America back from Alabama, Riley Smith. The order that followed: Pirates, halfback Bill Shakespeare (Notre Dame); Dodgers, fullback Dick Crayne (Iowa); Cardinals, halfback Jim Lawrence (Texas Christian); Bears, Stydahar; Packers, guard Russ Letlow (San Francisco); Lions, guard Sid Wagner (Michigan State); and Giants, tackle Art Lewis (Ohio). Stydahar and Letlow were the only two first-rounders who one could say actually made it in the NFL.

In fact, only thirty-one of the eighty-one players drafted that day ever played professional football. The others were not interested in the low salaries being paid in those days. The fabulous Don Hutson of the Green Bay Packers, for example, was only earning $300 a game, and the famed Bronko Nagurski of the Bears got a paycheck of $400 per game. The highest-paid player on George Preston Marshall's Boston Redskins was tailback Cliff Battles, who would later be elected to the Pro Football Hall of Fame; he was grossing $210 a game.

Bert Bell, the formulator of the draft, failed to sign *any* of his draft picks and came away from it with only the tackle he got from the Bears for Jay Berwanger. (One notable name besides

Berwanger who chose not to play in the pros that first draft year was a highly touted end from Alabama by the name of Paul "Bear" Bryant.)

So unheralded was pro football in 1936, the first NFL draft got not a mention in the next day's *New York Times*. A few days later it merited a three-paragraph story on the fourth page of the sports section.

This first draft did not usher in formal scouting, however. Teams simply could not afford full-time scouts. And once a team found *the* prospect it wanted and drafted him, it was not always an easy task to get the player to join the pros. Sid Luckman, the Bears' Hall of Fame quarterback, who had starred as a tailback for Columbia back when that school won football games, gives a good insight into how it was done in those days. "In 1938, George Halas wrote me a letter saying he might like to have me play for him in Chicago. I answered it, saying I didn't have any desire to play professional football. . . .

"Then Coach Halas called our coach, Lou Little, who talked to me for him. . . . After that he came to New York to see Lou Little and the three of us got together. [Actually, the Bears were playing the Giants that Sunday at the Polo Grounds.] I reiterated that I hadn't the least interest in playing professionally.

"The Bears made a trade with the Pittsburgh Steelers, anyway, so as to end up with the first pick in the 1939 draft, and they took me. He came back to New York again and by that time I'd gotten married. We had a little apartment. He came over to visit with me and my wife, Estelle, at the apartment. Coach Halas was a very insistent man. Estelle made dinner for the three of us. Afterwards he made a very fair and equitable offer. . . . He had the contract with him, handed it to me, and I signed it. Then he walked around the table and kissed Estelle on the cheek. He sat back down and lifted up a glass of wine and said, 'You and Jesus Christ are the only two people I'd ever pay that much money to.' I think it was five thousand or six thousand dollars at the time.''

The draft quickly expanded, reaching thirty rounds by 1943. Only about 20 percent of those players drafted during the first two years of World War II, however, ever reported to an NFL team. Instead, most reported for military service. By 1943, it was expected that only about 5 percent of those selected in the NFL draft would be able to play, which is why the draft had so many rounds. In fact, World War II was such a drain on the league's human resources that in 1943 the Philadelphia Eagles and the Pittsburgh Steelers had to merge, and became known as the "Steagles." The following year the Eagles decided to go it alone, and so the Steelers linked up with the Chicago Cardinals (the new team went by the name of "Card-Pitt").

There were some shrewd drafters in those early days, most notably George Halas of the Bears and Wellington Mara of the Giants. There were also some who did not do their homework very well, such as George Preston Marshall, founder and owner of the Washington Redskins. Like most other owners, he relied on what he read about college players, and he did that in a kind of scanning fashion, as the following story illustrates.

In 1946, the flamboyant Marshall made UCLA running back Cal Rossi his first-round draft pick. Unfortunately for the Redskins, one of the magazines Marshall had read mistakenly listed Rossi as a senior when he was in fact a junior—which, of course, made him ineligible for the draft. Marshall did not discover this until after the draft. So the Redskins lost their number one selection that year, and Rossi went back to UCLA for his senior year.

Undeterred, Marshall drafted Rossi in the first round again the next year. After that draft, Marshall learned that Rossi had no desire whatsoever to play professional football and instead was intent on launching a career in the business world, a fact that all the other owners in the league had known before the draft. So the Redskins again lost their first-round pick.

After the war, things changed markedly for the NFL when *Chicago Tribune* sports columnist Arch Ward launched the All-

America Football Conference, a new professional league, to compete with the NFL. The AAFC began in 1946 with eight teams: the Cleveland Browns, San Francisco 49ers, New York Yankees, Brooklyn Dodgers, Los Angeles Dons, Chicago Rockets, Buffalo Bisons, and Miami Seahawks (the Baltimore Colts would replace the Miami franchise the following year).

The biggest effect was the sudden competition for talent and the resultant skyrocketing of players' salaries. The AAFC lured some exceptionally talented football players. The Browns signed quarterback Otto Graham, fullback Marion Motley, tackle and placekicker Lou Groza, guard Bill Willis, center Frank Gatski, and end Dante Lavelli; the Los Angeles Dons got Elroy "Crazylegs" Hirsch; the New York Yankees had tailback Ace Parker and tackle Frank "Bruiser" Kinard. All of these players would eventually make it to the Pro Football Hall of Fame.

Other notable names joining the AAFC were tailback Spec Sanders and halfback Frankie Sinkwich of the Yankees, tailback Glenn Dobbs and halfback Dub Jones of the Dodgers, end Mac Speedie of the Browns, quarterback Frankie Albert and fullback Norm Standlee of the 49ers, quarterback Angelo Bertelli of the Dons, and tailback Bob "Hunchy" Hoernschemeyer and tackle Wee Willie Wilkin of the Rockets.

The NFL was so concerned about the new league that it held its draft in total secrecy in order not to give the AAFC a ready list of players to seek out and sign. The AAFC did not conduct a draft that first year; rather, it managed to pluck talent with more-than-competitive salaries. In addition, there were only ten teams in the NFL in 1946, and there was an enormous amount of talent returning from military service added to that year's crop of college seniors. To give an idea of the AAFC's impact, forty of the sixty-six college all-stars that year signed with teams in the AAFC.

An example of how the new league altered the NFL salary structure can be seen in the negotiations with All-America halfback Charley Trippi of Georgia. In 1947, Dan Topping, owner of both the Yankees in the AAFC and the major league baseball Yankees, offered Trippi a football/baseball contract worth $200,000. Bill Bidwill, owner of the Chicago Cardinals in the NFL, came up with a package that totaled $100,000 for playing football and trying out with the Chicago Cubs baseball team. Trippi, preferring the already-established NFL, signed with the Cardinals, where he starred for nine years, and was eventually inducted into the Pro Football Hall of Fame.

The AAFC held its first draft in 1947. Three of the biggest names in college football were drafted by AAFC teams: halfback Glenn Davis of Army by the Los Angeles Dons, halfback Buddy Young of Illinois by the New York Yankees, and quarterback George Ratterman of Notre Dame by Buffalo.

Both leagues conducted secret drafts for three years until, with the AAFC financially foundering, they decided to merge, bringing to an end the ever-escalating salaries that were bringing teams to their financial knees in both leagues. Only three teams from the AAFC ended up in the NFL—the Browns, 49ers, and Colts. The others shut down shop.

As a result of the AAFC and the competition to get the best players, scouting became a fact of life. There was still a great deal of dependence on the recommendations of college coaches and assistant coaches and information gleaned from magazines and newspapers, but scouts from NFL teams were now showing up on college campuses, and not just on Saturday afternoons to take in a game.

Most of the scouts in the late 1940s and the '50s were part-timers who would work during the college football season and maybe the spring practice sessions. Many of them were also former players of the team they were scouting for.

The most serious and effective system of scouting during that era was conducted by the Los Angeles Rams under owner Dan Reeves. It was innovative, in that it was the first to reap players from small schools, who were ordinarily overlooked in those days. Such finds by the Rams included running backs Tank Younger from Grambling (the first black player in the NFL to come from an all-black college) and Vitamin T. Smith of Abilene Christian in 1949, fullback Deacon Dan Towler from Washington & Jefferson in 1950, tackle Andy Robustelli from Arnold College in 1951, defensive back Dick "Night Train" Lane from Scottsbluff Junior College in 1952, and tackle Gene "Big Daddy" Lipscomb, who had not played college ball and was discovered playing football in the military in 1953.

In 1960, two factors fueled the vocation of scouting. In the NFL, a franchise was granted to Dallas and the Cowboys were born. And another new league, the American Football League, was launched to compete with the NFL.

In Dallas, the first thing Cowboy owner Clint Murchison did was hire Tex Schramm as his general manager. Schramm had served as general manager of the Los Angeles Rams under Dan Reeves and was well aware of the value of scouting.

However, the Cowboys were not eligible for the 1960 draft because their franchise was awarded after it had already taken place. So the only avenue left to the Cowboys was to track down the most promising players who had *not* been signed by other NFL teams. The obvious problem was to determine who they were. Schramm went to his former employer, the Rams, to work out a deal. The Rams had compiled a vast amount of information about players who had signed and those who had not and were now free agents. Schramm paid the Rams $5,000 for the data on the players who were free agents. Then he turned that information over to the first employee he hired, Gil Brandt.

Brandt, a former part-time scout for the Rams and a full-time baby photographer, was given the title of director of player personnel. Over the next three decades, he would prove to be one of the most fastidious and innovative scouting directors in the history of professional football. And his methods would have a far-reaching impact on the way other teams in the NFL approached scouting.

As he explains, "When we started [in 1960], we didn't have a scientific way of doing it. We just wrote a report, and many times we didn't cover all areas of the players' strengths or weaknesses. Then we decided we had to have a form of some type that encompassed the characteristics of all football players. We knew there were certain characteristics in a football player—mental alertness, strength and explosion, competitiveness, quickness, agility, and balance. So we set up a form that had those characteristics on it with a nine-to-one rating scale. And we included on the form position specifics, the seven different positions, so that we had different things for a wide receiver than we would for an offensive lineman, different things for quarterbacks than for defensive linemen.

"By 1961, we approached it with a semblance of organization. Before, people just wrote things about a player, and that can be a bad thing. Some people are very talented writers, and other people are not, so what happens is the one who writes a real good report, well, his player is likely to be drafted over a player whose report was not well-written. So by spelling everything out, charting things, rating characteristics, we developed a system."

And of course, that system served Dallas well over the years, the Cowboys being a strong contender from 1965 on (they went to five Super Bowls during the Schramm/Brandt/Landry years). The other teams would eventually follow suit; they would have to if they wanted to remain competitive.

The other factor was a repeat of the NFL–AAFC battle of the late 1940s, only it was fiercer and much more financially draining. The AFL was a well-financed league that was offering professional football to a lot of cities that had not been host to it before, such as Houston, Oakland, and Denver. The only three cities where the AFL would go head-to-head with NFL teams were New York, Los Angeles, and Dallas. By 1963, however, the Los Angeles Chargers would be relocated in San Diego and the Dallas Texans would move and become the Kansas City Chiefs.

During the early 1960s, while the NFL and the fledgling AFL, each with its own formal draft, were heatedly competing for the prime meat coming from the nation's colleges, a new job was created in professional football circles. In the NFL it was referred to as "representative," but it became better known as "baby-sitter."

A team in the NFL or the AFL not only had to draft a player, but it had to keep him from signing with a team in the other league, and that's where salesmanship, wiliness, and downright chicanery came into play. To protect its status as the senior league, the NFL came up with a unique strategy. With the most coveted prospects, a baby-sitter—usually a scout or front office denizen—was assigned to stay with the sought-after collegian, not only to convince him of the wisdom of signing with the baby-sitter's team, but also to keep him away from any team in the AFL that might have a similar inclination to get the player's name on a contract.

And it often worked.

Lamar Hunt, owner of the AFL's Dallas Texans in 1962, found this out, to his eternal chagrin. He was most interested that year in obtaining the services of North Carolina State quarterback Roman Gabriel. So were the NFL Los Angeles Rams.

A few weeks before the 1962 draft, Hunt personally telephoned Gabriel in Raleigh. In a conversation alleged to have lasted forty-five minutes, the Texan chief extolled the virtues of playing in the AFL, living in Dallas, and becoming an instant starter. "I went through our whole offer, from signing bonus to the ramifications of the tax consequences—everything. He was genuinely interested, I could tell. Very sophisticated for a college senior, I thought. Listened to everything I had to say, asked a lot of good questions, and when I got off the telephone I felt sure I had a good chance of getting him."

He might have, that is, if he *had* talked to Gabriel. As it turned out, Hunt's fervent telephone pitch had been delivered to baby-sitter Elroy "Crazylegs" Hirsch, then in the front office employ of the Rams, who was down in North Carolina with the sole purpose of mollycoddling Roman Gabriel. Hirsch had answered the phone call, not Gabriel.

Discovering his mistake sometime before D-Day and learning that Gabriel was safely and surely ensconced in the Los Angeles Ram camp, Hunt did not waste a draft choice on him.

But all was not lost, and perhaps to prove that there is poetic justice in the sometimes primitive world of professional football, Hunt and his coach, Hank Stram, with no good quarterback prospect now available from the draft, decided to take a look at a quarterback who had been cast off by the Cleveland Browns, Len Dawson, and decided he was worth signing as a free agent. Dawson, of course, starred for Hunt for the next fourteen seasons and eventually made it into the Pro Football Hall of Fame.

Another baby-sitting story of note involved Ron Medved, a highly regarded halfback from the University of Washington. The Philadelphia Eagles wanted him and sent a baby-sitter named John Merrill out to Seattle to keep him company. Medved had plans to get married the Wednesday before D-Day, but that didn't deter Merrill. Merrill went to the wedding rehearsal, the wedding, and the reception afterwards with Medved. Merrill even went along with the newlyweds on their honeymoon to San Francisco, but, it is said, settled for an adjoining room. The Eagles drafted and signed Medved.

By 1964, there were about 125 baby-sitters plying their trade in the NFL. And by that year salaries erupted like Mount St. Helens. Before the AFL came into being, salaries in the NFL were in the range of $10,000 to $25,000. In 1964, Alabama quarterback Joe Namath signed a three-year pact for $400,000 with the New York Jets. A year later, running back/punter Donny Anderson of Texas Tech signed a package-contract with the Green Bay Packers for $600,000.

The NFL–AFL war brought about the birth of the scouting combines, as well as the hiring of full-time scouts. The evolution over the next three decades has been remarkable. Today the scouting combines keep serious tabs on about five thousand college football players and each NFL team spends upwards of $1 million a year on scouting alone.

For three years, from their sophomore through senior seasons, the players are charted, studied, and graded. The lucky ones make it to the walls of war rooms in the twenty-eight NFL cities, the luckier ones are invited to the National Invitation Camp by the NFL, and the luckiest, of course, are selected in one of the twelve rounds on D-Day.

THE SCOUTING CAMP

If you are one of the select, one that the National and BLESTO scouting combines rate as among the very best at your position, you will get a formal invitation. You will also get a round-trip airplane ticket, hotel reservation, meal money, and the chance to show off your body and football skills to all twenty-eight National Football League teams.

It is often referred to as the NFL rookie combine. But that is a misnomer, because less than a third of the 430 potential rookies who are in attendance will actually end up playing in a regular-season game for an NFL team. Many may be drafted and some will sign on as free agents, but only about 130 will ever forge a career in professional football.

The rookie combine, sometimes more accurately called the scouting combine, is officially pegged the National Invitational Camp, Inc. It is an NFL-sponsored event whose purpose is to give the player personnel directors, scouts, coaches, owners, trainers, and team physicians of all twenty-eight NFL teams a last look at the top of the crop before the draft. Held in early February, it is a closed-door event; the media, agents, and fans are not allowed to watch as the meat is measured, weighed, and tested.

The first of these camps was held in 1982 in Tampa, and has since been conducted in places as diverse as New Orleans and Tempe, Arizona. But for the last few years it has settled into the Hoosier Dome in Indianapolis, that billowy indoor stadium that looks from the outside like an enormous heap of Pillsbury Doughboys.

Inside, the hopefuls are tagged and numbered, then taken in groups by position—offensive linemen, defensive linemen, linebackers, defensive backs, placekickers, punters, wide receivers, running backs, and quarterbacks—through three days of testing and measurement under the scrutiny of the collective eyes of twenty-eight NFL teams.

This is the meat market personified.

This is the first day of it, 1991.

Inside the Hoosier Dome, it is surprisingly quiet. And relatively empty. Besides the players, there are probably no more than a few hundred in the more than sixty thousand seats in this cavernous stadium. There are player personnel directors, coaches, assistant coaches, scouts, a few team owners. The quiet is broken only by the calling of a player's name over the public-address system or the shriek of a whistle to start a player on his 40-yard dash. From the stands issue only quiet murmurs from those talking or an occasional burst of laughter as an old scout or assistant coach tells a tale from times past—and there are a lot of them told when these guys get together.

It is also a gallery of famous football faces: Don Shula is standing there just outside the end zone in a sport shirt and yellow slacks, looking as if he just stepped off the golf course; Al Davis is sitting in the stands, appropriately clad in a lightweight black leather jacket, chatting with one of his Raider scouts; Dan Reeves walks up the aisle, saying hello to just about everyone he passes; Bill Parcells is in Levi's, running shoes, and a somewhat garish cardigan sweater, sitting alone, staring intensely out at the hopefuls, presumably not yet thinking of the retirement from coaching he will announce a month or so later.

Michael McCaskey is there from the Bears, standing down on the field talking with his offensive line coach, Dick Stanfel, who had an illustrious career playing guard for the Lions and the Redskins in the 1950s. Bill Tobin is taking it all in from a seat on the 50-yard line, alone, making notes. His scouts are scattered throughout the stadium. The team doctor and trainer are elsewhere in the complex, where other groups of hopefuls are being given physicals.

Coach Mike Ditka is out in California playing golf, but is expected in the next day or two. He is not so much interested in watching a player go through the tests, the drills; he is always looking for the word from those who can spot the players who apply intensity and dedication and perhaps savagery to the game—players like Chuck Bednarik, Dick Butkus, Walter Payton, or, indeed, himself.

In all, eighteen members of the Bear organization will attend the 1991 scouting combine.

Only one group of players is taken at a time on the field, where each athlete is clocked in the 40-yard sprint or put through paces coming off the ball or moving laterally, diagonally, backwards, or tested for position skills.

The players, in shorts, T-shirts, and running shoes, sit around in small clusters, or stand in lines, waiting to be called upon to perform. There is little talk among them. Some are doing stretching exercises. There is an air of intensity, nervousness; there is no slap-on-the-back locker room jocularity here. They know that what comes out of this three-day pageant may well determine if they'll have a job in the business of playing football next year and, if they do, just how many numbers will be behind the $ on their salaries. They do not seem to notice the assistant coaches and good-old-boy scouts as they walk by rocking on arthritic knees and destroyed hips.

Not all choose to attend this meat market. In 1991, top prospect Raghib "Rocket" Ismail, the junior wide receiver and kick returner from Notre Dame, decided to shun it. What if, for some reason or other, he has a 40-yard dash timing poorer than what he has already been timed at, or he has trouble catching the ball that day, or the doctors pick up something that might be disturbing to the teams' coaching staffs? His place in the draft, which everyone figures to be number one, could drop considerably, and with it his value, translated into dollars and cents.

The year before, quarterback Jeff George from Illinois had an excellent rating based on his college career. As he admitted later, "I decided simply that I did not want to risk performing poorly at the combine." It paid off: He skipped scouting camp, ended up the first pick in the first round of the 1990 draft, and signed a megadollar contract with the Indianapolis Colts.

On the other hand, the same year George decided to forgo the combine, highly touted linebacker Keith McCants of Alabama, who did show up, left a a lot of doubts about the condition of his surgically repaired knee and dropped a number of notches when D-Day came along.

But for most, it is a chance to show what they can do and to improve their chances of being drafted or moving up in the round in which they will be taken.

All the action, however, is not necessarily in the Hoosier Dome. On the streets around it there are players moving here and there. They are wearing sweat suits and running shoes and they are markedly different from the average jogger; you can tell by the thick necks, which seem to just flow symmetrically from the head into the shoulders.

And they are in the hotel lobbies nearby—the Holiday Inn

across the street, the Hyatt Regency, the Westin. The NFL does not treat them like second-class citizens.

Scattered among them in the lobbies are the agents and lawyers, lurking about to find those prospects who have not yet settled on someone to represent them. Thom Darden, who played for the Cleveland Browns in the 1970s and is now an agent, is in the Holiday Inn lobby. He says of the camp, "I liken this to the choice of who you marry. This is one of the most formidable decisions a young man has to make." Then he adds, "Unfortunately, since you [agents as well as media people] are not allowed at the activities in the Hoosier Dome, this is the only place where you have an opportunity to speak to the guys you would like to interest in your services. You grab them as you can."

The scouting camp is spread over five days, with groups overlapping each other. Each player is there only three days, however. The itinerary, at least in 1991, is this:

Day 1:

Upon arrival at your hotel, you check in with combine officials and receive an information packet and workout gear.

Next you go to a local hospital for a chest X ray and, as it is noted in the combine guidelines, for X rays, *if applicable*, of past injuries. After three years of college football, quite a few players here need them. The hospital keeps very busy making films of knees, ankles, hips, shoulders, and other assorted parts of skeletal systems.

Back at the hotel, you are tested for knee strength. This is certainly one test in which you do not want to come up with a low score.

At the end of the afternoon, there is an orientation dinner, at which the athletes gather by position group. You meet those you will be competing against. Most say it is pretty hard to be real friendly when you know what is at stake, but most try.

Day 2:

You are awakened at 6 A.M., and your first duty is to submit a urine sample, which is sent off for a thorough urinalysis. Among other things, they are looking to see if there are any illegal drugs in your system, from cocaine to steroids.

After breakfast, you go over to the Hoosier Dome for a complete medical examination. Doctors and trainers from all NFL teams are in attendance. There is a lot of standing in lines. You are herded from station to station, the signs reading ORTHOPEDICS, BLOOD PRESSURE, VISION, HEIGHT & WEIGHT, HAND & ARM MEASURABLES (hand span and arm length) . . . . It seems the only thing you are spared is a proctoscopic exam.

Next you are put through various tests for strength and are charted for repetitions on the bench press.

Day 3:

You go to the Hoosier Dome for workouts. The players work out in three large groups, the first starting at 8 A.M., the second at 10 A.M., and the third at noon.

First on the agenda, however, is the taking of full-length front and back photographs; it's sort of like being booked at the local police station. Then you warm up and do stretching exercises on the field as a group.

You are tested for flexibility.

Then comes the 40-yard dash. You are timed twice. Times are also recorded in the 10- and 20-yard distances. This is important, because here everyone is timed under the same conditions. A defensive back from one school, for example, may have been timed at 4:6 by BLESTO the previous autumn, but it was on a day when he was running into a wind and the field was not in the best condition. A defensive back from another school may have been clocked at 4:3, but he had a strong wind at his back and the ground was perfect. At the Hoosier Dome, all factors are equal and the teams can obtain a more accurate comparative assessment.

It makes sense. Before the creation of the camp, there were a lot of factors that could really vary. In 1968, for example, the

Dallas Cowboys were quite interested in what appeared to be a very speedy wide receiver named Dave McDaniels from Mississippi Valley State. His clocking in the 40 was most impressive. So the Cowboys drafted him in the second round. It turned out he was not all that fast, having been clocked in college at a distance of 38 yards that was mistakenly measured as 40. He was, according to Gil Brandt, "about as fast as you would expect a linebacker to be." McDaniels did not catch a Cowboy pass that year, and that was the length of his pro career.

After the 40, you are put through on-field agility drills that correlate with the position you play. Quarterbacks throw different kinds of passes, centers snap the ball, punters punt the ball, things like that, but there is no offense–defense confrontations. These drills are conducted by position coaches from various NFL teams.

Next is the measurement of your vertical jump. Tucked off in a corner of the Hoosier Dome is an apparatus that has vertical plastic slats hanging from it, patriotically colored red, white, and blue. You stand below it and leap up and slap the slats. From the top slat you slap, the judge observing you can tell how high you can reach jumping from a standing position. It is charted right there next to your height and weight.

Your jumping does not end here, though. Next it is over to another corner, where you are judged on the distance you can achieve in the standing broad jump. One defensive lineman from Oklahoma this year, standing in line, drawls, "What the hell's this for, to see if I can *jump* into somebody's backfield?" The guy next to him, from Penn State, says, "Well, you gotta get in there some way."

Then you are timed in the 20- and 60-yard shuttles to test your mobility.

There's one more activity. You perform four square cone drills, another mobility test. This means you run ten yards straight ahead, ten yards to the right, ten yards backpedaling, and ten yards to the left.

The report form looks like this, duly noting any injuries that prevent a player from performing a particular drill or test. These forms are provided to everyone in attendance for their own use.

When the scouting combine is over, each NFL team is provided with compiled results of the testing, as well as videotapes of each player's on-field drills.

And the potential pros pack up and go back to their schools . . . and wait . . . for D-Day.

THE MEAT MARKET

	1991			10 PUNTS		
Player Name	School	Event Jersy		Touch To Toe	Distance	Hang

ALSBURY, PAUL — SOUTHWEST TEXAS STATE UNIV — KP10

#	Touch To Toe	Distance	Hang
1	7	7	7
2	8	8	8
3	9	9	9
4	10	10	10
5	-Average-	-Average-	-Average-
6			

BLANCHARD, CARY — OKLAHOMA STATE UNIVERSITY — KP07

#	Touch To Toe	Distance	Hang
1	7	7	7
2	8	8	8
3	9	9	9
4	10	10	10
5	-Average-	-Average-	-Average-
6			

COBB, CHRIS — KANSAS STATE UNIVERSITY — KP11

#	Touch To Toe	Distance	Hang
1	7	7	7
2	8	8	8
3	9	9	9
4	10	10	10
5	-Average-	-Average-	-Average-
6			

FITE, JEFF — MEMPHIS STATE UNIVERSITY — KP12

#	Touch To Toe	Distance	Hang
1	7	7	7
2	8	8	8
3	9	9	9
4	10	10	10
5	-Average-	-Average-	-Average-
6			

GARDOCKI, CHRIS — CLEMSON UNIVERSITY — KP22

#	Touch To Toe	Distance	Hang
1	7	7	7
2	8	8	8
3	9	9	9
4	10	10	10
5	-Average-	-Average-	-Average-
6			

GREENFIELD, BRIAN — PITTSBURGH UNIVERSITY — KP13

#	Touch To Toe	Distance	Hang
1	7	7	7
2	8	8	8
3	9	9	9
4	10	10	10
5	-Average-	-Average-	-Average-
6			

HERTZOG, GREG — WEST VIRGINIA UNIVERSITY — KP14

#	Touch To Toe	Distance	Hang
1	7	7	7
2	8	8	8
3	9	9	9
4	10	10	10
5	-Average-	-Average-	-Average-
6			

NATIONAL INVITATIONAL CAMP, INC. : Day: | Group: 04 | Scout: 07 JOHN FITZPATRICK | Arrive: | Depart: | Position: DL | 02-04-1991

Player Name	School Name	Event Pos / Devls Pos	Ht.	Wt.	50th Reps	10 Yard	ET	20 Yard	ET	40 Yard	ET	VJ	BJ	20	Shuttle 60	4 Sq
LOGAN, ERNIE	EAST CAROLINA UN	DL11	DE													
MILBURN, DARRYL	GRAMBLING STATE	DL12	DE													
MILLER, COREY	SOUTH CAROLINA U	DL13	DE	LT KNEE SCOPED												
OLLISON, TONY	ARKANSAS UNIV -	DL14	DE	NO LIFT - FRAC LT FOREARM												
RICHARDSON, HUEY	FLORIDA UNIVERSI	DL15	DE													
RICHARDSON, TRAVIS	WASHINGTON UNIVE	DL16	DE													
SANFRATELLO, MIKE	NORTHERN ARIZONA	DL17	DE													
SHOWELL, MALCOLM	DELAWARE STATE C	DL18	DE													
SINCLAIR, MICHAEL	EASTERN NEW MEXI	DL60	DE													
SWANN, ERIC	BAY STATE TITANS	DL65	DE	SOFA												
WALKER, KENNY	NEBRASKA UNIV -	DL19	DE													
YOUNG, ROBERT	MISSISSIPPI STAT	DL20	DE													
ANDERSON, LE ANDRE	NEBRASKA UNIV -	DL64	DT													
DAHL, BOB	NOTRE DAME UNIVE	DL63	DT													
FRIDGE, GENE	USC - SOUTHERN C	DL30	DT													
GIANNETTI, FRANK	PENN STATE UNIVE	DL31	DT													
GIBSON, DON	USC - SOUTHERN C	DL32	DT													

LIVING
WITH
PLAN B

The NFL's Plan B, in which designated players are left unprotected and therefore are free to negotiate with other teams, can have a definite effect on the way a team will draft in April. Begun in 1989, it is a controversial program designed by the National Football League to deflect antitrust charges regarding free agency.

In effect, a team designates certain players it is willing to part with, making them unconditional free agents, on the February 1 before D-Day. If the player is not signed by another team by April 1, the rights to him revert to his original team. And if it does not sign him by April 15, the player becomes a free agent again. He cannot be paid less than his previous year's contract earnings. A team can protect no more than thirty-seven players, although it can protect less, and many do.

So here is an opportunity to shop around for veteran players before the draft. Some teams subscribe to the plan wholeheartedly. In 1990 the Green Bay Packers signed thirteen Plan B free agents from other teams, the New York Jets twelve, and the New

England Patriots eleven. It did not appear to help, however. The Patriots ended up with the worst record in the NFL, 1–15–0, and the Jets and the Packers were 6–10–0, both ending up in fourth place in their respective five-team divisions.

The Bears, however, are not one of the teams that subscribe to the plan. They have signed only one Plan B player in the three years of the program—guard Kurt Becker, who was a sixth-round draft choice of the Bears in 1982 but had been waived by them in 1989. Becker was picked up by the Los Angeles Rams and then left unprotected by them in 1990, at which point the Bears reacquired him. (Becker retired after the 1990 season.)

Bill Tobin is not overly fond of the program. He likes to build the Bears essentially from the draft. "We have been accused of not working at it [Plan B]. We have been accused of being afraid of it. We have been accused of disliking it, and that might be the only accurate statement. I dislike it because I think there are flaws in it. I think it breeds soldiers of fortune, or mercenaries. I don't think it promotes loyalty. I like our players better than we like some other team's players that are thirty-eighth or fortieth on their rosters."

It appears that other teams like Bear players better than some of their own, too. In the first year of the program (1989), the Bears lost nine players through Plan B, the following year seven, and in 1991 three.

"We speak to each of the players we are putting on Plan B beforehand and let each one know if we want them back," Tobin explains. "Sometimes we do it with more than words. [Linebacker] Jim Morrissey, for example: This year [1991] we improved his contract before putting him on Plan B. Plan B is the reason we are attempting to redo or renegotiate the contracts of some of our players."

Tobin may not like the Plan B program, but he and the Bears do not ignore it, either. As he explains, "Last year [1990] there were four hundred and ninety players on Plan B. We studied and reviewed every one of them.

"There is a lot to be taken into consideration. There are injury factors, there are salary factors, ability factors, character factors, size factors, condition factors—all kinds of things.

"We can live with the system. Ken Geiger [the Bears' official pro scout] has been working overtime to improve our Plan B approach. As a point of fact, we have been upgrading our Plan B information on everybody in the league. When February 1 rolls around, we are ready to go. As soon as we get a name, we sit down and look at Geiger's report, and we can tell pretty well right off whether we have any interest in the guy.

"We targeted twenty-seven players in 1990. Of those twenty-seven players, we reduced the list to about fifteen and started calling and making contact with them. Some of them were interested and some of them weren't. We ended up bringing in the ones who chose to come in for physicals. That's the main reason we brought them in, for physicals, and some of them failed the physical.

"Others did not meet our expectations when we saw them physically. They were forty pounds heavier, maybe, than what we remembered them weighing two years ago in college, for example. Some of them chose not to sign with the Bears because of the competition here. Some of them chose not to sign here because the dollar amount was better, perhaps, somewhere else. Out of the twenty-seven we initially targeted, we signed one."

The Bears admit to having made serious overtures to two players that year, however. One was fullback Tony Paige of the Detroit Lions, who was wanted as a backup for Brad Muster, but Paige chose to go with the Miami Dolphins. So the Bears drafted running back James Rouse from Arkansas that year and converted him to a fullback. The other was tight end Bob Mrosko of the Houston Oilers, because the Bears were unsure of how their own

Cap Boso would come back from the ankle surgery he had undergone just the month before. Mrosko opted, luckily for him, to go with the New York Giants instead, and went on to win the Super Bowl with them.

In 1991, the Bears were interested in speedster wide receiver Jamie Holland, whom the Los Angeles Raiders had put on Plan B. But Holland—at the last minute and after verbally agreeing to a contract with the Bears—decided to go back to the Raiders. Money had something to do with it. It prompted coach Mike Ditka to speak his mind on Plan B: "It is a farce, it is a joke. You jeopardize your whole ball club's pay schedule to take a fringe player that you have no certainty will help your football team."

In 1989, the first year of Plan B, 619 NFL players were left unprotected and 229 changed teams, but only 135 were under contract on opening day. Of the 490 NFL players set free in 1990, 184 changed teams, but by opening day only 110 had been signed.

Plan B transfers have so far proven that they usually have little, if any, effect on the success or failure of a team in the NFL. As the headline in *Pro Football Weekly* capsulized and captured it:

GIVE ME YOUR INJURED, YOUR OLD, YOUR SCRUBS—
THAT'S WHAT PLAN B IS.

There have, however, been some exceptions to this rule. In 1990, for example, the Miami Dolphins signed fullback Tony Paige of the Detroit Lions and linebacker Cliff Odom from the Indianapolis Colts, and both helped Miami get into that year's playoffs. And both were still there on the opening day roster for 1991.

On the other hand, the Los Angeles Rams, in need of a strong, veteran running back, lured longtime Seattle Seahawk Curt Warner and paid him a very hefty salary and signing bonus, only to find he was all washed up. It left them with only one decent running back, Greg Bell; and the Rams, who the year before had run all the way to the NFC championship game, ended up with a record of 5–11–0 in 1990.

San Francisco signed safety Dave Waymer from the New Orleans Saints for $700,000. He filled in effectively when Ronnie Lott was injured and was an instrumental factor in the decision to leave Lott unprotected in 1991.

The Cleveland Browns spent even more on cornerback Raymond Clayborn, $900,000, but with a different result. The generous salary so upset two of Cleveland's Pro Bowl veterans, linebacker Clay Matthews and cornerback Frank Minnifield, that they held out and did not join the team until after training camp. The Browns dropped from a division-winning record of 9–6–1 in 1989 to a cellar-dwelling 3–13–0 in 1990.

You win some, you lose some.

The Bears in 1991 took a serious look at about twenty players on Plan B, although they did not add a single one. They were highly interested in one player, however—defensive end Eric Kumerow, a three-year NFL veteran, a former All Big Ten defensive end from Ohio State, and a native of the Chicago area. They circumvented the February 1, 1991, Plan B deadline by trading defensive back Vestee Jackson to the Miami Dolphins for Kumerow on January 31, 1991.

As Don Pierson, sports columnist for the *Chicago Tribune*, explained it:

> The Eric Kumerow Vestee Jackson trade gave the Bears and Dolphins an alternative to the Plan B market. It also may have deprived both players of salary hikes.
>
> Both teams claim Kumerow and Jackson were going to be protected before they worked out the trade. But the NFL Players Association calls it another example of collusion to restrict player movement.
>
> "One more brick on the wagon," said Doug Allen, assistant executive director of the NFLPA. . . .

"This is the first time in the three years of Plan B that the trading period opened before the Plan B period. It gives teams a chance to swap unwanted players instead of bidding for them. Had Kumerow been a Plan B free agent, the Bears probably would have had to compete with other teams for him. Now they can pick up the final year of his contract, which paid $294,000 last season, and avoid the recruiting and signing bonus.

"He would have had some market value and now he has none," Allen said. "That is illegal conduct, and I'm sure it will be challenged."

Well, the illegality or the challenge asserted by Allen notwithstanding, the trade stood. Kumerow, however, spent the entire 1991 season in plainclothes instead of a Bear uniform, having ruptured his Achilles tendon against the San Francisco 49ers in Chicago's second preseason game.

Ordinarily the Plan B players are, to say the least, the lesser-knowns, often the youngest and the yet unproven. But they can also include the oldest on a team's roster, the over-the-hill players with the big salaries. The younger players may be definite future prospects who the team might like to keep to see if they develop into front-line players, and sometimes the "over-the-hill" guys are not quite over it. Both the younger players' development and the veterans' experience and proven ability may come back to haunt the team that put them on Plan B.

In 1991, there certainly were some major names on the Plan B rolls. The San Francisco 49ers surprised everyone when they set free perennial All-Pro safety Ronnie Lott and Pro Bowl running back Roger Craig. There was more than mild speculation that no one would pick them up because Craig's contract for the next year called for a $1.5 million salary and Lott's was at $800,000. The speculators were wrong, though; the 49ers' neighbors down the coast, the Los Angeles Raiders, signed both of them. The 49ers also freed linebacker Keena Turner, cornerback Eric Wright, and wide receiver Mike Wilson. Lott, Craig, Turner, Wright, and

Wilson were the only active players besides Joe Montana to have played on all four 49er Super Bowl champion teams, in 1981, 1984, 1988, and 1989.

The New York Giants put the previous year's Super Bowl Most Valuable Player, running back Ottis Anderson, on the list, along with tight end Mark Bavaro and defensive back Dave Duerson (who the Bears had, to many a surprised eye, cut in 1990). Anderson, approaching thirty-four, took it in stride. "You have to put me on Plan B. Dave Meggett, Maurice Carthon, Rodney Hampton, Lewis Tillman—they are the future running backs of the New York Giants." Nevertheless, Anderson was back in a Giant uniform in 1991. Bavaro, who was unable to come back from his injuries, retired, and Duerson, who the Giants were uninterested in keeping in the first place, was cut.

The Buffalo Bills left wide receiver James Lofton unprotected; the Philadelphia Eagles put former Bear quarterback Jim McMahon and wide receiver Mike Quick on the selling block.

Other NFL household names that surfaced on the Plan B list for 1991 included tight end Ozzie Newsome of the Cleveland Browns, guard Billy Ard of the Green Bay Packers, running back Greg Bell of the Los Angeles Raiders, quarterback Steve Grogan of the New England Patriots, kicker Pat Leahy of the New York Jets, nose tackle Jim Burt of the San Francisco 49ers, and guard Russ Grimm and running back Kelvin Bryant of the Washington Redskins.

Age and the budget . . . age and the budget . . .

After April 1, most of the big-name players who had been Plan B free agents were back in the fold of the teams they had played for the year before. By the time opening day of the 1991 regular season rolled around, James Lofton was catching passes for the Bills; Jim McMahon was back with the Eagles, and then throwing passes for them after Randall Cunningham suffered a season-ending injury; Pat Leahy was kicking the ball for the Jets; and Russ Grimm was blocking for the Redskins.

61

From Plan B the Bears, according to Bill Tobin, had been most interested in "offensive linemen, speedy wide receivers, corner-backs, and perhaps a punter." They apparently did not find one worthy enough or worth the price tag that would accompany him to Chicago, because nary a single Plan B player was signed by the Bears in 1991. So, as they much prefer to do anyway, Tobin, Michael McCaskey, and Mike Ditka focused their concentration on the upcoming draft.

In regard to that, the Bears also had to take into consideration the fates of the fifteen players they had left unprotected. Among them, the most well-known name was many-time All-Pro defensive tackle Dan Hampton, who had already announced his retirement. There was also quarterback Mike Tomczak, who had lost his starting job to Jim Harbaugh the year before. Finding his name on the list was no surprise, however, because it had been leaked to the press and media earlier that he would be there and also that it was unlikely the Bears would keep him even if he were not picked up by another team.

Other players left unprotected were guards Kurt Becker and John Wojciechowski, tight end Cap Boso, punter Maury Buford, defensive backs Maurice Douglass and James Lott, wide receivers Glen Kozlowski and Tom Waddle, linebackers Jim Morrissey, Mickey Pruitt, and Glennell Sanders, defensive tackle Terry Price, and running back Lars Tate.

On April 1, all returned, with the exceptions of Dan Hampton and Kurt Becker, both of whom retired; Mike Tomczak, Terry Price, and Glennell Sanders, who were lost through Plan B; and Lars Tate, to whom the Bears chose not to offer a contract. Of those returning, all made the final 1991 roster except James Lott, who was maintained as a member of the Bears' practice squad.

A total of 139 players switched teams as a result of the 1991 Plan B program. As they had the year before, the Green Bay Packers collected the most Plan B free agents, thirteen, followed by the Cleveland Browns with eleven and the Minnesota Vikings, who signed nine. The teams that lost the most players were the San Diego Chargers with eleven and the Miami Dolphins and Atlanta Falcons, who lost ten each.

From the players' (and their agents') perspective, there were some definite winners and losers, too. The biggest winner was tight end Alfredo Roberts, who moved from Kansas City to Dallas, where the money-ladling Cowboys increased his salary from $97,000 a year to $561,000 (plus a $150,000 signing bonus), a whopping 480 percent increase. One other player increased his wages by more than 400 percent, defensive end Jeff Faulkner, who the Phoenix Cardinals signed for $563,000, a 463 percent increase over the $100,000 the Indianapolis Colts paid him the year before.

At the other end of the salary circus, the largest decrease in pay went to Pro Bowl running back Roger Craig, whose $1,370,000 salary (contracted to increase to $1.5 million in 1991) with the San Francisco 49ers was pared to $775,000, a 43 percent cut by the Raiders.

Among the three Bears leaving Chicago, there were two winners and one loser. Defensive tackle Terry Price increased his earnings 213 percent when the Miami Dolphins upped his salary from $100,000 to $313,000. Linebacker Glenell Sanders, who had yet to play in an NFL game, rose from $76,000 with the Bears to $203,000 with the Los Angeles Rams. The loser was quarterback Mike Tomczak, who saw his $800,000 yearly take dwindle to $625,000 from the pocketbook of the Green Bay Packers, a 22 percent reduction.

As Bill Tobin later evaluated the 1991 Plan B transactions, "As far as I'm concerned Plan B was a success this year. We lost three players and got the rest of them back. We've got our thirty-seven core players still here. We have a good nucleus to go to [training camp in] Platteville [Wisconsin] with right now, and that's without signing any Plan B. We did attempt to sign Plan B players. There were five-hundred-plus available; we went through every one of them, shrunk it down to twenty-five; we shrunk that down further to sixteen; we made some telephone calls and found out a lot of players didn't want to come here because we protected five running backs or our offensive line was set or whatever reason they gave.

"We finally ended up bringing in seven or eight, gave them physicals, talked to them. We made an offer to one [Jamie Holland of the Raiders], who had agreed to it verbally, and were close with another [cornerback Charles Dimry, who instead went with the Denver Broncos], but on April 1 we were still sitting here with a goose egg.

"I think the success comes from the fact that our players are now understanding that the grass is not always greener on the other side of the fence and they are more willing to stay here and compete with our players, knowing our style of operation is more of a family style, more of a loyalty style—'you take care of me, I'll take care of you' attitude. Viewing Plan B in retrospect, I think we spent our money in the right place."

7

WINDING DOWN ... OR WINDING UP

April 1 is a Monday in 1991, and it is the start of the countdown to D-Day, at least in Chicago. The scouts for the Bears have arrived over the weekend and are ensconced at the Marriott Lincolnshire, their home for the next month or so—Rod Graves from Decatur, Georgia; Jim Parmer from Abilene, Texas; Charlie Mackey from Salt Lake City, Utah; Jeff Shiver from Lafayette, Indiana; Don King from Sun Lakes, Arizona. Ken Geiger commutes from his home in Berwyn, Illinois.

They assemble at Halas Hall that Monday morning, meeting essentially with Bill Tobin; have a few words with Michael Mc-Caskey and a few more with some of the assistant coaches who are at headquarters that day; and then get down to work.

At this point, there are approximately a thousand names that could appear on the wall in the war room adjacent to Bill Tobin's office. Only twelve will be drafted by the Bears, maybe twenty-some signed as free agents and given the opportunity to try to make the team.

The order for the draft is set. Four teams will not have first-round draft choices in 1991. The New York Jets gave up theirs when they took wide receiver Rob Moore in the supplemental draft the previous summer. The Indianapolis Colts gave up theirs when they traded up with the Atlanta Falcons the year before so they could obtain quarterback Jeff George. And the Dallas Cowboys obtained the first-round picks of the Minnesota Vikings when they sent running back Herschel Walker there and the New Orleans Saints when they dealt quarterback Steve Walsh to them. So, with those four teams out of it, this is the way the 1991 draft stacks up.

1. New England Patriots
2. Cleveland Browns
3. Atlanta Falcons
4. Denver Broncos
5. Los Angeles Rams
6. Phoenix Cardinals
7. Tampa Bay Buccaneers
8. Green Bay Packers
9. San Diego Chargers
10. Detroit Lions
11. Dallas Cowboys (from Minnesota Vikings)
12. Dallas Cowboys
13. Atlanta Falcons (from Indianapolis Colts)
14. Dallas Cowboys (from New Orleans Saints)
15. Pittsburgh Steelers
16. Seattle Seahawks
17. Houston Oilers
18. Cincinnati Bengals
19. Philadelphia Eagles
20. Washington Redskins
21. Kansas City Chiefs
22. Chicago Bears

23. Miami Dolphins
24. Los Angeles Raiders
25. San Francisco 49ers
26. Buffalo Bills
27. New York Giants

But it will not stay that way, not with what will prove to be one of the wheelingest-dealingest drafts in NFL history. The 1991 draft will go down as the year of the trade.

Before the scouts had even arrived, New England had already contacted the Bears, and Bill Tobin had relayed to Michael Mc-Caskey and Mike Ditka the Patriots' wish to trade the number one pick of the 1991 draft. The cost will be very high, perhaps two number one picks and other considerations (which could mean an established player or several later-round choices).

The newspapers are saying, however, that New England has a lock on Raghib Ismail—that its draft chief, Joe Mendes, is one of the Rocket's biggest boosters. It is said he believes Ismail is one of that rare ilk who can make the dazzling play, garner headlines, add a certain sheen to an otherwise lusterless team, and, most importantly, be a box office attraction who will bring the fans back to Sullivan Stadium in Foxboro, as well as to the television screens in the Boston area and around the country, on the Patriots' behalf.

Plus, New England is notorious for snatching wide receivers. No other team in draft history has ever taken a wide receiver as the number one pick besides the Patriots, who selected Irving Fryar in 1984. In fact, the Patriots have selected wide receivers in the first round seven times since that position evolved in the early 1960s: Gary Collins in 1962, Art Graham in 1963, Ron Sellers in 1969, Darryl Stingley in 1973, Stanley Morgan in 1977, Fryar, and Hart Lee Dykes in 1989.

Inside the Bear quarters, the talk is different. They, of course, know New England is shopping Ismail. Even this early, though, three weeks before the draft, the Bear triumvirate is in agreement that they do not want to trade up for him. And scouts Jim Parmer and Rod Graves both feel they might not even want the Rocket at choice number 22 if certain other players are still available. "I don't think they [New England] can afford him under the circumstances," Bill Tobin says.

The conversation now centers on whether someone else will meet the price. The Cowboys, Michael McCaskey suggests; after all, they have three draft choices in the first round. A possibility, all agree. The Raiders; one never knows what Al Davis might do on D-Day. The 49ers and Redskins; the way they throw the money around, who knows? But despite the conjectures, it all boils down to the fact that the Bears are not interested.

They kick around the idea whether there might be someone else for whom they could trade up, get the first pick, and forget the Rocket. But the price appears too exorbitant for any other player. It is not exactly the most tempting of draft years, they agree, in terms of available meat—one must remember that besides the top pick the year before, Jeff George, eight other juniors went in 1990's first round, depleting a lot of the meat that would ordinarily have been available in this year's draft. Jim Parmer quotes the Philadelphia Eagles' personnel director, Joe Wooley, who said, "It's the weakest draft I've seen in seventeen years. I'd have to say it's erratic."

Tobin talks to the effect that it is likely there will be someone left from the Bears' wish-list when number 22 comes around. He never really likes talking trade.

At this point, however, the Bears are still not ruling out moving up to a slot higher than number 22 if they believe the player they want will not last, and, of course, if the price is right. Other teams have called; there are deals offered, or at least suggested. Each is discussed.

The Bears traditionally have shied away from the trade just before D-Day or on the day itself, although they certainly listen and sometimes do some calling of their own. In regard to trading, Bill Tobin takes a posture that is pretty much diametrically opposed to that of the late George Allen, who brought the "Over-the-Hill Gang" to the Washington Redskins in the 1970s. According to Tobin, "There's a character risk as well as an injury risk. You might be getting somebody else's problems. When you try to trade yourself into a championship, you can be sucked down quickly."

Allen did, however, turn the tide for a losing Washington Redskin franchise in his seven-year tenure there and took the Skins to the playoffs five times and the Super Bowl once. One would not necessarily say Allen traded down in the draft; he traded *out* of it. His first year in Washington, 1971, he traded away his first, third, fourth, fifth, eighth, and seventeenth picks. In 1972, he gave up Washington's first *seven* selections. Each of the next three years, Allen traded away the club's first *eight* picks as well as assorted later selections. And in 1977, before being dismissed, he relinquished Washington's first *nine* draft choices. In fact, as a result of Allen's wheeling and dealing, the Skins did not have a first-round selection until 1980 (when they were perceptive enough to pick wide receiver Art Monk).

In any case, the talk of trade involving the Bears has not disappeared. Now, two weeks before the draft, Mike Ditka says, "As far as 1991 is concerned regarding trades, there has been some groundwork laid; by that I mean if someone wants to listen or we want to listen or they want to talk. But that is something we haven't done very much of. I don't know if we are good at it. We might get tricked if we try to do something like that."

And Bill Tobin said at the same time, "I think the chances of moving up in the draft are remote right now. Our needs are offensive linemen and defensive linemen, and we think there are some that will be there when we draft, some that we could be quite happy with.'' And he added later, ''When you're drafting in the twenty-second position, well, you can uncover a ruby the others have overlooked.''

The reason being—the Bears have great faith in their scouting program, their cross-check analysis (a top player will ordinarily be ''seen'' by three representatives from the Bears: the scout covering the area, another scout cross-checking, and Bill Tobin personally), and their own system of grading.

And they have always done well with their first-round selections. Their eleven first-round draft choices since 1983 are all starters in the NFL, nine on the Bears and two elsewhere (Willie Gault with the Los Angeles Raiders and Wilber Marshall with the Washington Redskins). Not only that, they have done exceptionally well drafting late in the first round, where they will be drafting in 1991: fullback Brad Muster was the twenty-third choice in 1988 and wide receiver Wendell Davis was twenty-eighth that same year, quarterback Jim Harbaugh was the twenty-sixth player taken in 1987, All-Pro running back Neal Anderson was twenty-seventh in 1986, defensive tackle William ''Refrigerator'' Perry was twenty-seventh in 1985, and wide receiver Willie Gault, who played for the Super Bowl XX champion Bears but was lost to the Raiders through free agency, was chosen eighteenth in the 1983 draft.

The Bears also have their favorite schools. Since the draft began in 1936 and prior to the 1991 draft, the Bears had chosen 1,105 players from 246 different colleges. The most popular is Notre Dame with 34 draftees, followed by Ohio State (24), Stanford and Texas (22), Illinois, Northwestern, and Oklahoma (19), and Arkansas (18).

The Bears have been somewhat predictable as well. In the fifty-five years of the draft, they have selected twenty-three running

backs in the first round, among them George McAfee, Gale Sayers, Walter Payton, and Neal Anderson (not too shabby), eleven
offensive linemen, and eleven defensive linemen; the rest are scattered among the various other positions. Only once have they taken
a tight end (Mike Ditka in 1961), a cornerback (Donnell Woolford
in 1989), or an offensive guard (Roger Davis in 1960).

A running back does not seem to be among the priorities in
1991, however, at least in the first few rounds. As coach Mike
Ditka explained at a press conference in the first week of April,
"We have said that we would kind of like to get a lineman
somewhere up front, offense or defense. We're not unhappy with
our people. We just know to stay up there you have to keep
replacing people. It is not a situation where we would draft a
person and put him on the field tomorrow. But we have to be
practical. We have some age in some areas and we have to be
realistic about it."

Bill Tobin agreed, noting that the Bears already had grades on
some offensive linemen that were as high as that accorded to the
previous year's Richmond Webb, a tackle out of Texas A & M,
who was drafted in the first round by the Miami Dolphins and was
so good his rookie year that he got an invitation to the Pro Bowl.
On the other hand, Tobin observed, "With Dan Hampton's retirement and Fred Washington's sad death and the loss of Terry
Price through Plan B, we certainly need people on the defensive
side of the ball."

Whoever it is that the Bears decide upon in Round 1, however,
they will not be able to pull off the coup they did the year before.
That was when they signed safety Mark Carrier of Southern Cal
to a contract *before* they took him as the sixth pick in the first
round of the 1990 draft.

About a week before that draft, the Bears had dispatched an
assistant coach to Los Angeles to talk with Carrier and his agent,
Jeff Irvin. They negotiated a contract that was finalized the day of

the draft. The Bears had actually talked to two other potential draftees about signing before the draft as well, defensive end Ray Agnew from North Carolina State and linebacker James Francis of Baylor, but neither were interested in the novel proposal. They were drafted later in the first round, the tenth and twelfth picks respectively.

The Bears came up with the idea after they had been stung the year before when their two first-round draft choices, cornerback Donnell Woolford and defensive end Trace Armstrong, were holdouts and missed most of training camp, considerably decreasing their initial value to the team. As Bill Tobin stated with more than normal emotion back in 1990, "We're tired of people accepting three-, four-, or five-year contracts and not being productive in the first year because they held out and stayed out of camp."

The before-draft signing ploy was not without controversy. Many other teams hailed it as good business, an innovative move on the part of management. The owners looked on it as a way to control the ever-escalating salaries of first-rounders, which has the residual effect of upsetting the salary structure of a team. You pay a top, but unproven, rookie as much as a guy who has gone to the Pro Bowl five times, and the veteran is not going to be happy with the contract that he'll now feel he is "saddled" with. In effect, prenegotiation and presigning can control inflation in the National Football League. Needless to say, many agents were less than thrilled with Chicago's maneuver.

Other considerations also arose. For example, what if a team drafting *after* the Bears persuaded the player to say no to the Bears because it would offer him more money even though it would take him farther down in the draft? Agents were thrilled with that aspect of it.

As George Young, general manager of the New York Giants, put it, "I think there is nothing wrong with what the Bears did. But from a competitive standpoint, it could cause us difficulty. I don't think it's good to have a lot of people talking to all the guys in the first round. It makes me nervous. We need rules to protect us from ourselves. I'd like to think everybody is ethical in this league . . . but I'm too old.''

Jim Finks, president of the New Orleans Saints and chairman of the NFL's Competition Committee, added, ''Potentially it could be a real problem. The draft is meant to disperse talent, not to create a situation to see who can pay the most money.'' The committee headed by Finks proposed a rule to NFL commissioner Paul Tagliabue that would prevent a team from talking to a potential draftee about a contract (that is, money) until its fifteen-minute decision period on D-Day.

In 1991, the Dallas Cowboys were counting on the ploy. They had *three* first-round selections. Dallas owner Jerry Jones went public and announced he wanted to get all three picks signed in time for mini-camp, not just training camp in the summer. This, he said, was a requirement—he wanted signed contracts before his three first-rounders were officially chosen on D-Day.

The volatile Jones said the Cowboys might negotiate with as many as ten or fifteen players before or on D-Day. That, he said, would eliminate the ''holdout posture'' (a new term in NFL jargon) and benefit both the club and the ballplayer. Jones and sidekick/coach Jimmy Johnson were already into discussions with Rocket Ismail and his agent, which Jones hoped desperately to work out so as to deal the super-speedster away from the New England Patriots and steal him from the lustful Toronto Argonauts of the CFL. Jones, it is reported, wanted the deal signed and sealed *before* formally addressing either the Patriots or the Argonauts, although he was maneuvering with one (New England) and doing his utmost to fend off the other's (Toronto) advances to Ismail.

Finks's rule, however, was adopted, and Jerry Jones and perhaps the Bears and a lot of other teams had to readjust their strategies. According to the rule, teams could still make nonfinancial inquiries to a player or his agent, things like how the player felt about playing in a particular city or under a particular coach. But as of early April 1991, no team could talk money or sign a player prior to its fifteen-minute time period on D-Day. It became known as the "Carrier Rule."

The ploy had certainly paid off for the Bears. Carrier went on to set an all-time Bear record and lead the NFL in pass interceptions with ten, was named the league's Defensive Rookie of the Year, and went to the Pro Bowl. He was the first Bear rookie to go to the Pro Bowl since defensive tackle Wally Chambers did after the 1973 season, and the first defensive rookie to start all sixteen games since defensive tackle Dan Hampton did in 1979. The only other Bears in history to have earned NFL Rookie of the Year honors have been tight end Mike Ditka in 1961, Ronnie Bull in 1962, and Gale Sayers in 1965.

But there were to be no followers in this adroit move. The "Carrier Rule" prevailed.

Back at Halas Hall in Lake Forest, the scouts gather around the conference table in the war room. At this point there are no lists on the wall. They won't go up there until they are whittled down and the final Bear grade has been given for each player. The reports on the players are there, however—the BLESTO report, the scout's report, the cross-check report, Tobin's report. If the player went to an all-star or bowl game, there is a report on that. There is the information gathered at the National Invitational Camp in Indianapolis on performance as well as physical condition. The only thing missing, it seems, is an FBI report.

The procedure, according to Bill Tobin, who composes, orchestrates, and conducts it, is this: "We sit down together as a group, just myself and the scouts at this point, our own reports in front of us, all the other reports handy. For no reason other than tradition we start with the fullbacks, then the running backs, quarterbacks, receivers, tight ends, offensive linemen. When we finish the offense we go through the defense, position by position, then the kickers and punters.

"We start with the fullback who has the highest BLESTO rating and work our way down through the fullbacks in the order in which they have them. Then we move on to the next position . . . and the next, and the next."

Tobin reads the BLESTO report on its top-rated fullback, then reads from his own notes from the two meetings he has had with the BLESTO people during the year on all the higher-rated players (meetings on lesser players are unlikely). The information gleaned from the National Invitational Camp is discussed and added to the player's profile.

The next step is for the scout who has followed the player to read his report. "I encourage them all the time," Tobin notes, "to not just read from their reports but to ad-lib opinions or give asides if they have them. They can spark discussion, maybe add some insights." Then the scout who has cross-checked the potential draftee reads his notes.

The scouts discuss the player in a variety of lights at this point. For example, if there was a significant weight gain between junior and senior year, it might indicate he was on steroids. They might discuss the possibility of this particular player being lured off to the Canadian Football League, or perhaps to major league baseball—everybody knows Bo. A definite consideration is the degree of difficulty there will be in signing him; who his agent is can be a distinct concern.

This is also the time the scout can do a little lobbying for the players he is highest on. Rod Graves, the Bears' assistant director of player personnel and a practiced scout himself, is well aware that the scout's job is a selling job. "Coach Ditka relies strongly on the scouts' observations and their opinions, and, of course, on those of Bill Tobin. He does not have the time to take away from his job to watch all that much film of all the players under consideration."

And scout Jim Parmer corroborates: "I think you're not a very good scout if you don't sell your people—I mean the ones you're interested in. Just having a grade on him doesn't really mean a whole lot—you've got to push for him. You're not helping your ball club if you don't.

"The Refrigerator [the Bears' sometimes 340-pound, sometimes 380-pound defensive tackle William Perry] is a good example. We didn't have agreement he was a first-round player and a couple of us had to talk like hell to get McCaskey to take him. You see a lot of times the kids in the, say, twentieth to twenty-eighth picks have really second-round grades, but if you take them in the first round then you have to pay them first-round wages.

"I remember Jerry Vainisi [the Bears' general manager in 1985] saying to me, 'How much do you like this kid?' 'A lot,' I said. 'Then you better sit down over there next to McCaskey and start talking your tail off to him.'

"A number of the people weren't super-high on him. Ditka liked him. Some others didn't. He was awfully tough to grade. I'd been over to Clemson and talked to his position coach there, a fella I knew from when he was at Oklahoma State. He told me about Perry. 'The biggest thing you're going to have to watch about him is his appetite, which is enormous,' he said. 'Let me give you an example,' he said. 'One day we had a real hard two-a-day workout and we just worked his ass off. Well, he went home and had his wife go out and buy six chickens, and he ate every piece.' I said that's got to be a goddamn lie, nobody can eat six chickens. But it weren't no lie. He also had a deal with McDonald's down there [Clemson, South Carolina]. You see, he was easily the most visible person in town. So McDonald's would let him come in about twelve-thirty at night, just when they were closing, and what they hadn't sold they'd give to him. Sometimes he'd eat as many as twenty hamburgers a night.

"I can usually tell within ten pounds of a guy's weight, but with this guy I had no idea. He looked the same to me at three-forty as he did at three-eighty. But I liked what I saw in him, and I talked for him; so did a couple of others, and we ended up taking him in the first round that year (1985, twenty-second pick).

"Actually, we were probably going to take this safety out of Texas, a kid named Jerry Gray who the Rams grabbed the pick before us. So when he was gone we convinced McCaskey that Perry was the best available. That's the way it goes sometimes."

It is indeed. And William Perry added a whole new dimension to the term "refrigerator" around Chicago.

After all the reports are read and the roundtable discussion completed, Bill Tobin puts a final Bear grade on the player, which can vary considerably from the one given him by BLESTO. According to Tobin, the procedure can take from about fifteen minutes for the better-rated players down to as little as five for the lower-rated ones.

Those minutes add up to a lot of hours when you are talking about perhaps a thousand football players.

About a week, but sometimes as little as three days, before D-Day all the meat has finally been graded. The fat has been trimmed and approximately five hundred names remain for posting on the wall of the war room at Halas Hall.

THE MEAT, 1991

Nowadays, the method of judging the collegiate meat that is worthy of playing in the National Football League has become such a systematized process of gathering and interpreting data that it deserves its own scientific name—perhaps "draftology" would be appropriate, putting it right up there with biology, geology, meteorology, and all the other ologys.

It is a far cry from the simpler days when owners like George Halas and Bert Bell and Art Rooney and George Preston Marshall worked the draft headquarters themselves, with the help, perhaps, of their head coaches.

The atmosphere was far different, too. George Halas in his heyday of after-dinner speeches liked to tell stories about the relaxed nature of those earlier drafts. They were usually held in the city where the NFL championship game was played, sometimes the day after, sometimes the day before. All the owners and coaches were there, so they would not have to come up with carfare to another city at another time.

Halas remembered that, between picks, it was not out of the ordinary for Jimmy Conzelman, then the coach of the Chicago

Cardinals, to go over to a piano in the hotel conference room and entertain the others with a song or two, or to see Pittsburgh Steeler owner Art Rooney hustle to the closest pay telephone to get a bet down on a horse he had suddenly developed a fondness for.

And, according to Halas, the owners were not above a little practical jokery. A memorable one involved George Preston Marshall, who was never known as being a shrewd or even well-informed drafter for his Washington Redskins, but was universally well known for his unfailing dedication to the spirit of segregation. (The Redskins, under the bigoted Marshall, were the last team in the NFL to bring a black player aboard, and that was not until 1962, and not until the NFL forced him to do it.) At one draft in the early 1950s, Marshall made his selection, and Steve Owen, longtime coach of the New York Giants who was sitting nearby, looked over and said, "George, do you know he's a colored boy?"

An aghast Marshall shouted toward the lectern, "Commissioner, Commissioner, wait a minute . . ." but he was drowned out by the laughter coming from those at the tables around him, the heartiest of them from the accomplished joker Owen. His coach, seated next to him, assured Marshall that his choice was pure white. "Never mind, Commissioner," the relieved Redskin owner said.

Halas also later admitted to a little chicanery of his own in those days—leaving papers and notes strewn about the Bears' table just before the draft was to start and then taking whoever was with him from the Bears out into the hall for an apparent huddle. The paperwork contained the misinformation he wanted to pass on to those left in the room, who would invariably file by to sneak a peek. "All's fair in love, war, and football" was a motto Halas subscribed to.

In those days professional football was a game that was played incidentally for money. In the 1990s it is a business and a science that is played incidentally as a game.

79

With all the research, reports, computer printouts, systems of grading, intelligence information, physical profiles, films and videos, the procurement of players for the NFL teams is today essentially a depersonalized one. The Bears rarely talk to a player they are highly interested in during the time he is being scouted and assessed, Bill Tobin admits. "The college coaches don't want you or the scouts to; they want their kids to have their minds set about college football, not to be distracted. They're a pretty big business themselves. But we don't need to talk to them. I don't even want to."

Michael McCaskey adds, "That's why so many of our players are surprised when we draft them, especially the first-rounders. [Offensive tackle and future All-Pro] Jim Covert was surprised, [linebacker] Wilber Marshall was surprised, [fullback] Brad Muster was surprised. Maybe the most surprised of all was [quarterback] Jim Harbaugh."

Harbaugh had reason to be surprised when he was drafted in 1987. The Bears had drafted only one quarterback in the first round in the preceding thirty-six years—Jim McMahon of Brigham Young in 1982, the first since Notre Dame's Bob Williams in 1951.

And it might have remained that way had Mike Ditka gotten his way. That year, Ditka wanted to take defensive end/linebacker Alex Gordon of Cincinnati in the first round. "He was arguing like hell for him in the draft room that day," Jim Parmer remembers. "Tobin said he would be happy with either one of them. But a lot of us, including McCaskey, were worried about [starting quarterback] Jim McMahon's injuries. He seemed to be getting hurt more and more each year.

"Well, it finally boiled down to McCaskey saying to Ditka, 'Let's go into my office.' When they came out, McCaskey said we were going to take the quarterback. Mike [Ditka] said, 'I don't give a shit who you take; I probably won't be here to coach him anyway.' Then he stomped out of the room, but he came back in about an hour and everything was fine."

Despite all the technics involved in scouting and drafting these days, the players are still human and the game is still played with intense emotion. The teams that prevail do so because of the talents, efforts, and attitudes of their players.

The Bears like to look at it this way. What they are after in a football player are the three Ms: Meat, Mental ability, and Moral character. Not that all their ballplayers are or have been adroitly drawn composites of King Kong, Alfred Einstein, and Mother Teresa, but the team does, according to McCaskey, "look well beyond just the physical aspects and the previous performances of people we seriously consider to draft."

There have, of course, been a variety of instances over the years of behavioral problems: Bulldog Turner and Bobby Layne being arrested for peeing in an alley outside a nightclub one night in 1948, their photos in jail appearing, to the ultimate chagrin of owner/coach George Halas, in one of the next morning's newspapers; the fabled off-field antics of gigantic defensive end Doug Atkins in the 1950s and '60s (tackle Fred Williams: "We had a martini-drinking contest. I drank twenty-one, same as Atkins. But he beat me; I figured, because he drove me home and carried me in, that he must have won."); Jim McMahon, *enfant terrible* of the 1980s, with his mouth and the emanations that came from it and such whims as mooning a helicopter just before Super Bowl XX in January 1986; and the drunken-driving arrests of several Bear personnel in recent years.

In the last decade, however, in comparison with other NFL teams, the Bears have been closer to choirboys than gangsters. As Ray Sons, sports columnist for the *Chicago Sun-Times*, wrote in an April 1991 article, "The Bears almost never mix football and felonies. This does not happen by chance. We must thank Bill Tobin, his scouts, Mike Ditka, and president Mike McCaskey, for seeking character references. Their top draft choices turn out to be big on visiting hospitals, preaching to troubled kids, and raising money for charity.''

And the past decade of the Chicago players' performances on the field bear testament that their wholesomeness has in no way adversely affected their play on the green fields of professional football.

As Bill Tobin explains, ''We're very careful, but it doesn't make us immune. We go to great lengths to assess character. We study the potentials from various points of view. For example, do they treat the janitor in the same way they treat the head coach? We don't just take the head coach's or position coach's opinion about this guy's character; we check with the equipment manager who washes the guy's socks. We ask how they treat people. You run into players who act one way with a person of position and another with an ordinary guy on the street. It tells a lot about his character and how he will perform under the rigors and stress of pro football. We look for people who act the same in all situations. It matches Mike Ditka's and the Bears ownership's profile . . . we look for attributes that go beyond merely the measurements by scale or stopwatch.''

This philosophy gives an insight into what Tobin calls the player's ''Bear profile,'' and it will be a pervasive factor in the player's ''Bear grade.''

The prescient Ray Sons ended his April 1991 article with this observation: ''My guess is his [Bill Tobin's] first choice will be an eventual replacement for one of the team's offensive linemen. Whoever this draftee is, history tells us he will be more likely to show up in the Pro Bowl than in a police lineup.''

The Bears of the 1990s would never draft a Joe Don Looney, for example, no matter what his playing credentials were. George Halas might have—after all, he took by trade the notorious Doug Atkins after Paul Brown at Cleveland admitted he could not handle the raucous defensive end—but the McCaskey-era Bears would not even entertain the notion.

Looney, who many around the NFL said was the most appropriately named player in the league, was one of the finest running backs in college football as a junior (1962) at Oklahoma and an awesome punter who could boot the ball sixty yards in the air. As a senior, he failed to practice and upset his teammates with his attitude and quirks so much that they asked their coach, Bud Wilkinson, to remove him from the team, and Wilkinson, who by that time was as frustrated as the players, complied.

The New York Giants, however, decided to take a chance on Looney and selected him as their first-round choice for 1964. Wellington Mara would much later say it was the most unfortunate first-round choice in the franchise's history. Looney did not even make it through the first training camp before beleaguered coach Allie Sherman and Mara shipped him off to Baltimore in a trade. During his brief stay with the Giants, he refused to read the team's playbook and told Sherman, "A good back makes his own holes. *Anybody* can run where the holes are."

Looney had a peripatetic career in the NFL, going from the Giants to the Colts to the Lions to the Redskins to the Saints, contributing little to any of those teams. He has one distinction, however: He is the only first-round draft choice in the history of the NFL to have taken a job tending elephants in India after ending his pro football career.

Looney, of course, is not the only first-round draft choice to have been a bust in the pros. The Bears, although considered one of the better-drafting teams over the years, have had their share. The most regrettable, perhaps, was tailback Bob Fenimore in 1947.

Fenimore was a great all-around back who could run, pass, and catch with the best of the collegians of his time, which included players like Glenn Davis, Doc Blanchard, Johnny Lujack,

Charley Trippi, Doak Walker, Bobby Layne, and Bob Chappius, to name just a few.

The year 1947 was the first year of the Bonus pick, in which each team drew from a hat for the first choice (the team with the worst record, therefore, getting the second choice). That first year, the Bears, coming off a championship season, and Halas, with the luck of the Bohemians, drew the Bonus and took Fenimore.

But Fenimore proved to be injury-prone and lasted only a year with the Bears before retiring forever from the playing field.

In 1951, there was Bob Williams, a quarterback out of the Bears' favorite school, Notre Dame, who sat on the bench for three years and so soured the Bears on taking a quarterback early in the draft that they did not take one in the first round again until Jim McMahon in 1982. Then there was halfback Billy Anderson in 1953, out of Compton Junior College in California, whose only claim to fame, as it turned out, was that he was the son of the actor who played Rochester on the old Jack Benny radio and TV programs. And who could forget halfback Ron Drzewiecki from Marquette (1955), end Tex Schriewer of Texas (1956), halfback Don Clark of Ohio State (1959), center Dave Behrman of Michigan State (1963), defensive end Loyd Phillips from Arkansas (1967), or running back Joe Moore of Missouri (1971)?

Well, they may not have left their impression on the Bears or NFL history, but since 1975, the Bears, in the first round, have drafted with a deftness that is the envy of the rest of the league. Look at the list not only of starters, but of Pro Bowlers:

1975 Walter Payton (running back, Jackson State)
1976 Dennis Lick (offensive tackle, Wisconsin)
1977 Ted Albrecht (offensive tackle, California)
1978 (traded pick to Cleveland)
1979 Dan Hampton (defensive tackle, Arkansas)
       Al Harris (defensive end, Arizona State)

1980 Otis Wilson (linebacker, Louisville)
1981 Keith Van Horne (offensive tackle, Southern Cal)
1982 Jim McMahon (quarterback, Brigham Young)
1983 Jim Covert (offensive tackle, Pittsburgh)
   Willie Gault (wide receiver, Tennessee)
1984 Wilber Marshall (linebacker, Florida)
1985 William Perry (defensive tackle, Clemson)
1986 Neal Anderson (running back, Florida)
1987 Jim Harbaugh (quarterback, Michigan)
1988 Brad Muster (fullback, Stanford)
   Wendell Davis (wide receiver, Louisiana State)
1989 Donnell Woolford (cornerback, Clemson)
   Trace Armstrong (defensive end, Florida)
1990 Mark Carrier (safety, Southern Cal)

Finding college talent that will make it in the pros, all scouts will agree, is not as easy as it looks. In some cases, it is, however. As Jim Parmer points out in regard to the Bears taking Walter Payton in the 1975 draft, "Hell, my mother could have pegged him, and she don't know a lot about running backs." Parmer, who scouted Payton when he played at Jackson State down in Louisiana, says, "Sometimes there's just a natural, kind of a rare gem you see in a handful of rocks."

On the other hand, there is the glitter of the would-be gems who have turned out to be nothing more than glass. The Heisman Trophy is the highest accolade that can be laid on a college football player, but Archie Griffin, a great running back at Ohio State and the only collegian to have ever won the illustrious award twice (1974 and 1975), proved to be nothing more than a journeyman in the NFL with the Cincinnati Bengals. He ground out maybe four hundred or so yards a year and never really brought a crowd to its feet as he routinely had in Columbus, Ohio, when Woody Hayes was smiling and Ohioans were cheering.

And what about the Heisman quarterback club of winners who

all flopped in the NFL? The first was Angelo Bertelli from Notre Dame, who won the Heisman in 1943. The first pick in the first round of the 1944 draft by the Boston Yanks, then an NFL franchise, he had a two-year hiatus from football because of World War II and, after it, ended up with the Los Angeles Dons in the newly formed All-America Football Conference (AAFC). A knee injury soon ended his career.

After Bertelli, there was another Notre Damer, Johnny Lujack, the Bears' first-round choice in 1946 (he was a junior at the time), who joined the team in 1948. As good a defensive back ("one of the best I ever saw at that position," George Halas said) as he was a quarterback (to this day he still holds the Bear record for passing yardage in a game—468, then an NFL record, in 1948 against the archrival Chicago Cardinals), Lujack succumbed to a shoulder injury and never became the star everyone expected him to be.

And then there was Terry Baker of Oregon, Heisman of 1962, first-round draft pick of the Los Angeles Rams in '63 who, because he could not pass well, was converted into a running back. He lasted three lackluster years before moving on to a career in law.

An equally undistinguished NFL career was that of Notre Dame quarterback John Huarte, Heisman of 1964, who flitted about the league (he was drafted by the New York Jets of the AFL in 1965, then was shuffled to the Boston Patriots, Philadelphia Eagles, and Kansas City Chiefs before his curtain-closing year, 1972, with the Bears).

Gary Beban, who took the Heisman in 1967 after a great career at UCLA, during which he passed for more then four thousand yards, was drafted by the Los Angeles Rams in 1968. He completed one pass in his two-year NFL career.

In 1971, Auburn quarterback Pat Sullivan earned the Heisman. He was drafted in the second round the following year by Atlanta, where he sat on the bench for four seasons, playing behind such quarterbacks as Bob Berry, Bob Lee, and Steve Bartkowski.

Doug Flutie of Boston College won the Heisman in 1984, but is perhaps best remembered for a desperation pass he threw sixty-four yards in the air for a game-winning touchdown against Miami. The game was called "The Battle of the Quarterbacks" by one sportswriter, and "The Battle of Mutt and Jeff" by another (Flutie was 5'9½" and Miami's Bernie Kosar was 6'5"). The cannon shot that Flutie threw gave Boston College a 47–45 victory that day and clinched the Heisman for him. But the diminutive quarterback could not hack it in the NFL, spending most of a year on the sideline for the Bears before moving on to the New England Patriots and eventually the Canadian Football League.

Two other Heisman quarterbacks are in the game today. Vinny Testaverde, who was the number one draft pick in the first round of the 1987 draft, has been a disappointment to Tampa Bay, where he regularly throws interceptions and is routinely booed. Andre Ware, the ninth pick of the first round of the 1990 draft, sits on the bench for the Detroit Lions, a third-stringer.

Then there is the Outland Trophy, awarded each year to college football's outstanding interior lineman. For every such winner as Merlin Olsen of Utah State, Tommy Nobis of Texas, Ron Yary of Southern Cal, Randy White of Maryland, or Lee Roy Selmon of Oklahoma, there are such pro busts as Rich Glover of Nebraska, John Hicks of Ohio State, Brad Shearer of Texas, Jim Richter of North Carolina State, and Dave Rimington of Nebraska (who won the award two consecutive years, 1981 and 1982).

Still, the hunt goes on, and in the 1990s it is certainly a sophisticated one.

Because BLESTO's gradings are guarded about as closely as the CIA's roster of spies and are available to absolutely no one other than the subscribing teams (they are even sent out in code), we will use the gradings of the other combine, the National Scouting Combine, which apparently is not so security-conscious (its gradings by position appeared in the February 19, 1991, issue of *USA Today*, two months before the draft).

The grading system the National uses ranges from a high of 9.0 down to 4.0. It roughly translates this way:

8.5 to 9.0—should be a franchise-maker
8.0 to 8.5—should be a sure rookie starter
7.0 to 8.0—should start as a rookie
6.0 to 7.0—should be an eventual starter
5.0 to 6.0—should contribute as a rookie
4.0 to 5.0—a prospect worth drafting

Only seniors are graded here; the grading of juniors who have opted to forgo their senior year and enter the draft are speculations made by the author.

Fullbacks first.

Not a high priority on the Bear wish-list. It is also a position that is not all that well-stocked in 1991. The reason is that big-time college teams, like a lot of the NFL teams, are using one-back offenses. The Bears are not one of them. And therefore they could be interested in a big, strong-blocking fullback to back up Brad Muster and open paths for Neal Anderson, someone larger than James Rouse to challenge him for that backup job. But he won't be found in the early rounds of this year's draft. He'd have to be a sleeper, the unanimous opinion around the Bear camp is, someone taken deep down in the draft or picked up as a free agent, one who could perhaps later prove that BLESTO, the National, and the other NFL teams were victims of oversight. Maybe another Roland Harper, if Jim Parmer has one hidden away in his mind or one of the other scouts can come up with one.

The best at this position appears to be Jarrod Bunch of Michigan. He is big (6′1½″, 240 pounds), powerful, and known to be a very physical blocker. He also ran the 40 in 4:60. The scouting reports are that his pass-catching ability is so-so and that he is not an elusive runner. But then, most fullbacks aren't. The National graded him as the best fullback available, 6.3. So under the

National's system of grading, Bunch should be an "eventual starter." The now-defunct *National Sports Daily*, which lumped fullbacks with running backs in its list of the top pro potentials, ranked Bunch the sixth best back in the nation. His biggest asset, according to the Bears' Rod Graves, is his blocking ability. The Wolverines capitalized on that, using Bunch to lead the way for running backs like Jon Vaughn and Tony Boles.

The Bears know, however, they would not consider him in the first three rounds, and they pretty much accept the fact he won't be there after that—although stranger things have happened in the NFL draft.

There are others to consider who might be available later in the draft. There's Robert Wilson of Texas A & M, a 5'11½", 246-pound junior who wasn't graded by the National but who, it is speculated, would have come in somewhere in the vicinity of 5.8 to 6.0. Jim Parmer, who scouted him, sees him as a pile-driving runner and an excellent blocker, who was clocked at 4:83 in the 40. *The National Sports Daily* figured Wilson to be the seventh best back available in 1991.

After these, there are three others with good grades: Cedric Jackson of Texas Christian—6', 227 pounds, a 4:56 in the 40, and a rating of 5.5; Greg Amsler of Tennessee—a little over 6'2" and weighing 240, with a speed of 4:75 in the 40 and a rating of 5.41; and finally Walter Dean out of Grambling—a shorty at 5'10" and also a lightweight at 197, by far the least-loined of the available fullbacks, who ran the 40 in 4:64 and earned a rating of 5.4.

There is also the possibility of Nick Bell from Iowa, who is classified as a running back instead of a fullback but who, at 6'2" and varying between 250 and 259 pounds, could indeed fill the role of fullback. But there are some questions about him. For instance, although many believe he is the best running back/ perhaps fullback available, he is not an impact blocker, according to some scouting reports, and that is not a good credential in a

Ditka-designed offense that depends so much on the run from the tailback (or Neal Anderson) position.

There are other fullbacks on the board at Halas Hall. Each will get his hearing, albeit shorter than the ones received by the players just mentioned. These are the ones whose destinies truly rest in the hands of the individual scouts.

Only a few feet away from the fullbacks in the two-back offense, or alone in the increasingly popular one-back offense, are the running backs, one of the two true glamour positions in pro football—witness Gale Sayers, O. J. Simpson, Tony Dorsett, Walter Payton, Eric Dickerson . . . And they are only a few inches away from the fullbacks on the Bears' board.

The year 1991 is considered a relatively lean one in terms of running backs. There are some first-rounders here, it is speculated, and there seems to be a consensus of who the cream of the crop is—although the rank will vary depending on whether you are reading the BLESTO reports, the National reports, the individual teams' gradings, *Pro Football Weekly*, *The National Sports Daily*, *Sport* magazine, or some other publication.

These include Harvey Williams of Louisiana State, Nick Bell of Iowa, Aaron Craver of Fresno State, Eric Bieniemy of Colorado, and Leonard Russell from Arizona State.

The Bears have some pretty thorough reports on all five of them. Jim Parmer has watched Harvey Williams for a couple of years. Jeff Shiver studied Nick Bell. Don King will speak for both Aaron Craver and Leonard Russell. Charlie Mackey has covered Eric Bieniemy and can even pronounce his name correctly. But the Bears are not really interested in a running back in the first few rounds, although these five players still warrant serious discussion and they will get it.

Harvey Williams is a solidly built (6'1½", 212 pounds), powerful, upright running back who has been compared in style to Eric Dickerson. He ran the 40 in 4:46, the third swiftest according to the National, and received its highest grade, 7.21. He is said to have good running instincts, is an above-average pass-catcher and a good kick returner. Parmer's report, however, shows that Williams has been hampered by injuries. Parmer notes that Williams sat out the 1988 season because of a knee injury and that he is fumble-prone. "And with coach Ditka's heart condition," Parmer adds, "he don't really need a fumble-prone back."

Nick Bell is by far the biggest of the five at 6'2½" and a weight in the mid-250s. One report—not the Bears'—referred to him as the next Franco Harris, the Pittsburgh Steeler star of the 1970s. Another compares him favorably with Christian Okoye, the rhinoceros running back of the Kansas City Chiefs. Still another, however, notes that Bell was a "soft runner, one who does not pack a big wallop for his size." Bell has been timed as fast as 4:45 in the 40, although the National lists him at 4:54. He grades out second in the running-back category at 7.2. The Bears have heard, however, that he is an "underachiever." The Bears' Rod Graves thinks Bell is somewhat of a question mark in the pros. "He has size and speed, but he is not a workhorse, or at least didn't demonstrate that at Iowa." Talk around Halas Hall is that Bell will probably go in a round earlier than he should, and there doesn't seem to be much concern about that particular fact.

Aaron Craver is an unpolished, sometimes erratic runner, and says so himself: "I understand what they [the critics] say about me, because I have a tendency when I break into the open to head straight for the safety and try to run him over." On the other hand, his coach at Fresno State, Jim Sweeney, says Craver "maybe has the most potential of any player I've coached"—and he has coached Henry Ellard of the Los Angeles Rams and Stephone Paige of the Kansas City Chiefs. A good blocker, Craver is 5'11¼", 216 pounds, has run the 40 in 4:42 (4:51 according to the National), and is graded 7.01.

He was a walk-on at El Camino Junior College in Torrance, California, before enrolling at Fresno State. As Craver tells it, when he showed at El Camino the coach asked what position he played.

"Whatever position you need," Craver answered.

"We're kind of short at running back," the coach said.

"Well, that's the position I really wanted to play anyway."

The Bears rate Craver high and think he will go probably in the second round.

Eric Bieniemy is the midget of the group, 5'6¾" and 193 pounds. One scouting report, however, says he has "amazing power for his size, explosive quickness, and is very competitive." Still, there is some question about his pass-catching ability and a worry that he tends to fumble too frequently. The National has him clocked at 4:40 in the 40, the fastest of any back on its list, and graded him at 6.7. Bieniemy, a consensus All-America, was third in the Heisman Trophy vote, trailing only Ty Detmer of Brigham Young and Rocket Ismail of Notre Dame. He gained 1,628 yards rushing (the second most of any back in NCAA Division 1-A) and another 159 on pass receptions in the eleven games he played for Colorado his senior year.

Leonard Russell is a junior, and at 6'1½" and 237 pounds has been described as having the size of a fullback and the speed of a tailback (he has been timed at 4:76 in the 40). It is noted that he has had a persistent shoulder problem, which may not sit well with a lot of teams, but it tested out fine at the National Invitational Camp back in February. Because he is a junior, he has not been formally graded, but he would probably check in somewhere around 6.8. Don King, who scouted Russell, thinks he may be the best back available in the 1991 draft and that he might go in the first round.

It would be a surprise if any of these five will be around by the time the Bears are likely to take a running back, perhaps the second half of the draft. But there are others almost as highly regarded who might be: Ricky Watters of Notre Dame (6'1", 212 pounds, 4:48 in the 40, graded 6.01); Ivory Lee Brown of Arkansas/Pine Bluff (6'1½", 232 pounds, 4:54 in the 40, graded 6.6); Jon Vaughn of Michigan (a junior, 5'9½", 203 pounds, 4:50 in the 40, probably would grade out about 6.6); Blaise Bryant of Iowa State (5'11", 200 pounds, 4:55 in the 40, graded 7.0); Darren Lewis of Texas A & M (5'11", 205 pounds, 4:65 in the 40, graded 6.2); Ricky Ervins of Southern Cal (5'8", 190 pounds, 4:57 in the 40, graded 6.5); and James Joseph of Auburn (6'2", 222 pounds, 4:65 in the 40, graded 6.21). The Bears will read up on all of them . . . and others as well.

The other glamour position in professional football is quarter-back, of course. Quarterbacks traditionally command the biggest salaries, invariably get the most press and the most commercial endorsements. They are the names so indelibly left on the game: Sammy Baugh, Sid Luckman, Bob Waterfield, Otto Graham, Norm Van Brocklin, Bobby Layne, Y. A. Tittle, Johnny Unitas, Bart Starr, Joe Namath, Sonny Jurgensen, Fran Tarkenton, Roger Staubach, Terry Bradshaw . . .

At no other position, however, have more college superstars flopped in the pros. Of the fifteen quarterbacks to win the Heisman Trophy and join the NFL, ten have left little if any imprint on the league. One, Notre Dame's Paul Hornung, made it big (big enough to get himself into the Pro Football Hall of Fame), but he did it as a halfback on Vince Lombardi's legendary Green Bay Packers. Only one of the fifteen Heisman winners could be considered a certified star quarterback in the pros, Roger Staubach, who took the trophy at Navy in 1963 and later earned his way into the Hall of Fame playing for the Dallas Cowboys.

Notre Dame, which has had more than its share of bust quarterbacks in the NFL, has, on the other hand, also given us Daryle Lamonica, a twenty-fourth-round draft pick of the Buffalo Bills in 1963, who after being traded to the Oakland Raiders went on to have a fine twelve-year NFL career; and Joe Theismann, who played first in Canada, was acquired by the ever-trading George

Allen in 1974, and led the Washington Redskins for the next decade, including a victory in Super Bowl XVII in January 1983 and a loss in Super Bowl XVIII in January 1984; and Joe Montana, who was drafted in the third round in 1979 and proceeded to lead the 49ers to *four* Super Bowls, all of which they won, and is a sure shot for the Pro Football Hall of Fame when he finally ends a most illustrious career.

In 1991, however, there does not seem to be the lusted-after, promise-filled, franchise-making quarterback. There is no John Elway, Dan Marino, Troy Aikman, or Jeff George out there, and that feeling filters throughout the league. There are a few top prospects, first-rounders perhaps, but no first-magnitude stars, no big-card draws.

The Bears are not worried about their quarterbacking situation. It is youthful. Mike Tomczak, who lost the starting job to Jim Harbaugh and, left unprotected in Plan B, went with the archrival Green Bay Packers, is not missed. "I'm very comfortable with both Harbaugh and [Peter Tom] Willis," Mike Ditka says at the time, and he means it. "And I'm glad we have Brent Snyder [a member of the team's practice squad]."

Although coach Ditka is comfortable with the current quarterback ensemble, both he and Bill Tobin express the opinion that they would like to go into training camp in July with four quarterbacks, and that means they will probably pick one up in the later rounds of the draft or sign one on as a free agent after it.

The top three quarterback names bandied about the war rooms of the NFL in 1991 are Dan McGwire of San Diego State, Brett Favre of Southern Mississippi, and Todd Marinovich of Southern Cal. But it it rumored no team would be willing to trade up for any one of them.

At 6'8" and 235 pounds, McGwire looks like he might be more appropriately slotted as a forward in the NBA draft than as a quarterback in the NFL draft. He graded out best with the National, a rating of 7.0, but he had the slowest 40, 5:17, of all the quarterbacks the combine graded and is notorious for his lack of mobility. He is, in the words of one scout, "a classic drop-back passer, no Tarkenton, no [Steve] Young [the 49ers' scrambler]." But he has terrific arm strength and is considered an accurate and productive passer (he threw for 3,833 yards and a 60.1 completion percentage his senior year at San Diego State). His mobility problem may not hamper him all that much, a lot of the scouts feel, because the NFL has relaxed the in-the-grasp rule. As George Young, general manager of the New York Giants, put it, "It's ironic. We alter a rule to benefit mobile quarterbacks, and ultimately it may benefit a guy who everyone says is immobile." Dan is also the brother of Oakland A's slugger Mark McGwire, if that means anything.

Brett Favre ranked only fifth with National, 5.8, but a lot of other observers rank him the number one prospect, including *The National Sports Daily*, *Sport* magazine, and *Pro Football Weekly* (tied with McGwire). He has size—6'2½", 220 pounds—and runs the 40 in 4.90. He also has a highly respected arm, easily lofting sixty-yard passes or drilling the ball over the middle with pinpoint accuracy. One scouting report raves about his leadership on the field. But recently he had shoulder surgery and was involved in an automobile accident that resulted in his having a portion of his lower intestines removed.

Todd Marinovich, a junior and therefore unranked by National, could also go in the first round, but it would have to be to a gambling team, one unafraid of handling roguish ballplayers— say (and many did) the Los Angeles Raiders. He was arrested in January 1991 for drug possession and was suspended from Southern Cal for repeatedly missing classes. He was also suspended from the team after a number of run-ins with USC coach Larry Smith. "Troubled" is the adjective most associated with Marinovich. Still, he has the size (6'4", 218 pounds) and the arm (a 61.6 completion percentage over two years at USC). The Bears have no interest whatsoever in him.

There are also some other significant quarterbacks. The National ranks Paul Justin of Arizona State second to Dan McGwire, grading him out one point below the San Diego State star at 6.0. Justin is a relatively willowy quarterback at 6'3½" and 202 pounds who runs the 40 in five-flat. His scouting report says he has a strong arm and an excellent release; on the negative side, he separated his shoulder in his senior year.

Browning Nagle, whose name makes him sound like someone out of an F. Scott Fitzgerald novel, is from the University of Louisville via a transfer from West Virginia, and is considered a pocket quarterback with limited scrambling ability but a rifle arm. He has often been compared to the Buffalo Bills' stellar quarterback Jim Kelly . . . not bad company. At 6'2" and a weight that fluctuates between 220 and 235, Nagle is a big question mark, however, because he had an injury-filled senior season and suffered a shoulder injury in a postseason college all-star game.

There are other worthies. Craig Erickson of Miami (Florida) is one of the more fondly thought of—maybe not by the National, which ranked him sixth (5.5), but by others, although most were wary because he was just coming off knee surgery for an injury he incurred in practice before the Hula Bowl in January. Then there is Scott Zolak, a 6'5", 224-pounder from Maryland, who, a number of scribes think, is going to San Francisco, despite the fact that the 49ers already have Joe Montana and Steve Young. The National is not as optimistic, making him its eleventh-rated quarterback (5.1). There is no question he has a strong arm, and *Pro Football Weekly* noted he is so dedicated that he "studies more film than Siskel and Ebert."

Others considered draftable are Don Hollas of Rice (6'2½", 219 pounds, 4:75 in the 40, graded 5.9); Shawn Moore of Virginia (6'1¾", 4:66 in the 40, graded 5.4); and Bill Musgrave of Oregon, (6'2", 200 pounds, 4:86 in the 40, graded 5.2).

One of them will probably be taken by the Bears and given a shot to beat out Brent Snyder for the second backup quarterback slot. Then there is talk around Halas Hall that maybe they will just go with two quarterbacks in 1991 and keep a third on the practice squad.

Wide receiver is a position the Bears have a slightly more than ordinary interest in. Ever since they lost world-class speedster Willie Gault to the Los Angeles Raiders, they have not had the game-breaking blazer they could throw the bomb to and be relatively confident he had gotten a step or two on the defenders. Only problem, this does not seem the year of the Willie Gault–style wide receiver in the draft—excluding, of course, Rocket Ismail.

Wide receivers have not ordinarily been a high priority in the first round of drafts. Some of the greatest were not plucked until late or appeared without advance notice and wormed their way onto a roster through rookie free agency.

The Bears have drafted only two wide receivers in the first round since that position came into existence as such in the early 1960s: Willie Gault in 1983 and Wendell Davis in 1988, and they were eighteenth and twenty-eighth picks, respectively.

In the 1990 draft, no wide receivers were selected in the first round. Wide receivers may be the biggest gambles in the game, according to NFL personnel strategists. Michael McCaskey says they are "very hard to predict, predict in terms of how they will fare in professional football," and calls wide receivers "perhaps one of the most difficult positions to gauge, as difficult as their counterpoints, the defensive backs." George Young, general manager of the New York Giants, summed up the view of most NFL teams when he said, in regard to wide receivers, "If you have your druthers in the early part of the draft, it's the dance of the elephants. You get the smaller guys later."

There have been first-rounders like Lynn Swann, picked in 1974 by the Pittsburgh Steelers; Jerry Rice, taken by the San Francisco 49ers in 1985; and Sterling Sharpe, chosen by the Green Bay Packers in 1988. But over the years there have been a lot more busts taken at this position in the early rounds of the draft than there have been players who have made an impact.

Rod Graves says there is a lot of talent at this position in the 1991 draft, but he does not see the Bears taking a wide receiver in the first few rounds.

The National likes Reggie Barrett, who caught his passes for Texas–El Paso. Barrett and Notre Dame cornerback Todd Lyght are the only two players in 1991 to grade out at 8.0 or above, which means that they are the only two seniors the National considers sure starters as rookies. Barrett, with an 8.2, in fact, graded the highest of all players in National's system in 1991. Clocked at 4:53 in the 40, the 6'2½", 208-pound Barrett is far from the fastest wide receiver available, but he is strong and aggressive, according to some scouting reports. Joel Buchsbaum of *Pro Football Weekly* observed that Barrett ''is not a true burner and did not have a good senior season or Senior Bowl, but catches with his large, soft hands and makes some highlight-film plays.''

A lot of sources think Herman Moore of Virginia or Alvin Harper of Tennessee are the best available (Harper was graded third by National with a 7.02). Both are in the vicinity of 6'3", both weigh 205 pounds, both are fast, and both can high-jump more than seven feet. Moore caught fifty-four passes for 1,190 yards and thirteen touchdowns during the 1990 college season, and Harper set a school record with eight touchdown receptions as a senior and had an exceptionally good Senior Bowl.

Randal Hill of Miami (Florida), graded only twenty-fourth by National (5.34), is highly regarded by a number of sources. He is rated one of the fastest players by National, with a 4:42 in the 40. They say he makes up for his size (5'10½", 179 pounds) with his quickness.

The others garnering the most predraft attention include Jake Reed of Grambling, the National's second highest rated wide receiver (6'3", 216 pounds, 4:45 in the 40, graded 7.2); Derek Russell of Arkansas (5'11¾", 175 pounds, 4:45 in the 40, graded

7.0); Jeff Graham of Ohio State (6'1", 195 pounds, 4:51 in the 40, graded 6.81); Wesley Carroll, another Miami (Florida) receiver, (6'0¼", 183 pounds, 4:59 in the 40, graded 6.8); Ed McCaffrey of Stanford (6'4½", 195 pounds, 4:50 in the 40, graded 6.30); Anthony Morgan of Tennessee (6'0", 195 pounds, 4:50 in the 40, graded 6.01); Mike Pritchard of Colorado (5'9"¾, 182 pounds, 4:51 in the 40, graded 5.8); Tim Barnett of Jackson State (6'1", 209 pounds, 4:50 in the 40, ungraded); and juniors Rob Carpenter of Syracuse and Dave Daniels of Penn State.

The Bears have been talking about taking a wide receiver, but not until maybe the middle or late rounds because coach Ditka is quite satisfied with his current stock. "Ron Morris has the speed to run with most people," Ditka said. "He's not a burner but he is a very fast football player. Wendell Davis is basically the same way. . . . Dennis Gentry has given us great football for a lot of years." But the Bears will be looking, and their grades on wide receivers seem significantly different from those compiled by National, so it could be interesting.

It would appear the Bears might be in the market for a tight end after having left unprotected in Plan B both Cap Boso and James Coley, and protecting only James Thornton, but there is little talk of acquiring one. The reason for the seeming lack of interest may be because the pickings at tight end are slender in 1991.

The most prolific at catching passes is Chris Smith of Brigham Young, a consensus All-America his senior year. Graded at the top of National's sheet on tight ends (6.5), Smith has the height (6'3½"), but his 227 pounds is the second lightest on National's tight-end listing. He is 4:78 in the 40, according to National, but after a hamstring injury in a postseason all-star game he could do no better than 5:03 at the National Invitational Camp in February in Indianapolis. His blocking ability is questionable at best. A lot of teams have deep reservations about him, the Bears among them.

Reggie Johnson of Florida State rates second, according to National. He certainly bulks more than BYU's Smith—Johnson is 6'2", 257 pounds, and he is faster, 4:63 in the 40; his grade is 6.03. Johnson is also considered a punishing blocker.

Two other hulkers are Jerry Evans of Toledo (6'4", 244 pounds) and Adrian Cooper of Oklahoma (6'5", 250 pounds). Evans runs the 40 in 4:49 and grades 6.01; Cooper runs it in 4:85 and grades an even six.

Kerry Cash of Texas, in the eyes of some scouts, may be a sleeper. At 6'4", 230 pounds, he runs the 40 in 4:75, but grades only 5.6.

The general feeling among those who analyze the upcoming draft is that no tight end will go in the first round, and maybe not in the second either.

Bill Tobin, Mike Ditka, and Michael McCaskey are much more interested in the other fellows who play up on the front line with the tight ends—the offensive linemen.

Offensive linemen. As Don Pierson, sportswriter for the *Chicago Tribune*, once described them, "You can't win without quarterbacks and running backs and defensive backs and linebackers and receivers; you can't even start to think about it without [offensive] linemen.

"They are underpaid and eventually overworked, unappreciated and inevitably unhealthy. The linemen on defense get some glory; the ones on offense just get gory."

For NFL teams participating in the first round of the 1991 draft, it appears to be a grand year for offensive linemen. It is projected by a lot of folks that as many as five or six might go in the initial round. Bill Tobin agrees: "It is, in my opinion, the strongest area of this draft." This is also an area of special interest to Chicago, where age and injuries are catching up to the Bears' front line. And the Bears are not adverse to taking an offensive lineman in the first round—witness their current starting tackles, first-rounders Keith Van Horne (1981) and Jim Covert (1983).

They have five offensive linemen, graded highly, who they feel are worth drafting in the first round. As to which is the best, or perhaps most coveted, that depends on who you talk to at this point. The worry, the concern at this point, is who of those will be around by pick number 22 . . . or should they try to trade up to get one of them . . . or should they just let the old chips fall where they may and take the best available athlete. They talk about these alternatives a lot as the time winds down to D-Day.

Two of the most heralded offensive linemen played for the same team, the Tennessee Volunteers, and both are gargantuan tackles—Antone Davis and Charles McRae. Davis, at 6'4¾" and 317 pounds (he has played at 327), is the largest among the top ten or so linemen, and he is among the fastest, timed at 5:00 in the 40. Davis, who graded 7.5, can also play guard. Rod Graves, who scouted him for the Bears, says he would love to see Davis around when the twenty-second pick comes up, and so would Bill Tobin, but they both know he will not be there. There is a true consensus that both Davis and McRae will be gone within the first eight draft picks. McRae, who is a little taller and less bulky (6'6¾" and 291 pounds), is a former defensive linemen who is also considered quite adept at blocking field goals and PATs. McRae ran the 40 at 5:20 and graded at 6.9. The Bears are very high on McRae as well. But the only way they can get either one, they believe, would be to trade up. There has been talk of it around Halas Hall.

There are two other highly rated offensive linemen the Bears are very interested in—Pat Harlow of Southern Cal and Stan Thomas of Texas. They are both tackles, although Thomas has also played guard and is looked upon as usable at either position in the NFL. Harlow is the second-ranked tackle by National, grading 7.2; he is 6'5¾", 275 pounds, and runs the 40 at 5:10. Thomas is third, just ahead of McRae, rated 7.0. National has his weight at 290, but he is often over 300, stands 6'5‴", and was clocked at 5:30 in the 40. The Bears would be very happy if either is around when their turn comes up. Because there are four out-standing prospects at tackle alone, there is also talk around Halas Hall that trading up may not be such a great idea.

Even after that fearsome foursome of tackles, there are some worthy prospects. Kevin Donnalley of North Carolina is one: 6′5″, 295 pounds, 5:25 in the 40, and graded 6.8. Mark Vander Poel of Colorado is another. He specs out at 6′7½″, 304 pounds, a 5:31 in the 40, and a grading of 6.0. According to *Pro Football Weekly*, there is also a sleeper from the Ivy League, Joe Valerio of Penn-sylvania; the National grades this 6′¾″, 290-pounder at 5.51.

National's highest-rated guard is Eric Moten of Michigan State—that is, if you do not see Antone Davis or Stan Thomas converting full-time to that position. Moten, exceptionally strong and mobile, is 6′3″ and 292 pounds, runs the 40 in 5:10, and grades 6.8.

Ed King of Auburn is another well-regarded guard. He is a junior and therefore ungraded, but he checks in at 6′4″, 296 pounds, and a timing of 5:27 in the 40.

Other guards who have garnered attention include Hayward Haynes of Florida State (6′2″, 280 pounds, 4:78 in the 40, grad-ing 6.1); Stacy Long of Clemson (6′1½″, 274 pounds, 5:07 in the 40, grading 6.01); and Gene Williams of Iowa State (6′2¼″, 325 pounds, 5:31 in the 40, grading 5.5).

At center, Chris Thome of Minnesota heads the National list, and John Flannery of Syracuse is at the top of most everybody else's. Thome, according to scouting reports, can also play tackle or guard. How he stacks up: 6′4″, 276 pounds, a 5:10 in the 40, grading 6.9. Many scouts, however, think Flannery has much more defined skills in terms of strength, speed, smartness, and work habits. He is 6′3½″, 301 pounds, runs the 40 in 5:07, and is graded second by National at 6.01.

Also worth considering at the snapper slot are Mike Heidt of Notre Dame (6′2½″, 285 pounds, a 5:10 in the 40, and a grading of 6.0), Blake Miller of Louisiana State (6′1½″, 277 pounds,

5:01 in the 40, graded 5.3), and Mike Arthur of Texas A & M (6'4", 265 pounds, 5:15 in the 40, graded 5.2).

There is a lot of heft in the offensive-line prospects. The top college prospects of 1991 already outweigh the Bears' formidable front line, all of whom have proved to be of Pro Bowl caliber. Mel Kiper, the analyst for ESPN television, lists his top ten college tackles at tipping the scales between 285 and 318 pounds, with the average being 297. The top ten guards weigh in between 274 and 316 pounds, averaging 291. And the five highest-ranked centers range between 268 and 300 pounds, their average being 282.

It seems a long way and a lot of bulk from the days when comparatively tiny Hall of Famers manned the front line, like center Chuck Bednarik of the Philadelphia Eagles (6'3", 230 pounds), tackle Rosey Brown of the New York Giants (6'3", 255 pounds), tackle/guard Forrest Gregg of the Green Bay Packers (6'4", 245 pounds), and center Mel Hein of the Giants (6'2", 225 pounds).

Defensive linemen are also at the head of the Bears' wish-list. They are, in fact, at the head of almost all NFL teams' wish-lists. There just are not enough good ones to go around. According to the draft analysts and the scouting reports, each of them seems to have a serious shortcoming, including the top-graded ones.

The Bears are most interested in tackles, Bill Tobin has said. Mike Ditka has said publicly that he especially likes Notre Dame tackle Chris Zorich. Tobin notes that the choices may be at the semiprecious-stone level: ''There's no Bruce Smith [Buffalo Bills, out of Virginia Tech, drafted number one in 1985] or Reggie White [Philadelphia Eagles, out of Tennessee, taken in the supplemental draft of 1984]. But there are some solid players. Some aren't as tall as you'd like, or as fast, or are more suited as a nose tackle [which the Bears, in their 4–3 defense, have no use for.].''

Topping everybody's list at tackle is Miami's 6'1", 271-pound Russell Maryland. The winner of the Outland Trophy (honoring college football's most outstanding interior lineman), he received a National grade of 7.2. With a 4:98 in the 40, he is renowned for his quickness, intelligence, and technique. But he is only 6'1" and has short arms, and NFL coaches like their defensive linemen to be about 6'4". According to Tobin, "Most offensive linemen ideally are six-three to six-six. You like your defensive linemen to be as tall as the offensive linemen. But there are other factors." Most draft handicappers figure Maryland to be among the first eight picks, probably around fourth or fifth, despite his size.

National rates Moe Gardner of Illinois second, graded 6.8, but he has the same size problem as Maryland. He carries a mere 254 pounds on a 6'2" frame. He is fast, though—4:88 in the 40—and may perhaps be taken with the idea of converting himself to a linebacker.

Louisville's Ted Washington has the size (6'4½", 299 pounds) and grades out at 6.3, but he is not as quick (5:17 in the 40), and every scouting report notes his lack of motivation and his propensity for eating himself out of shape. Rod Graves, who scouted him for the Bears, underlined "underachiever" in referring to Washington.

Bobby Wilson of Michigan State is well thought of, grading out at 6.3. But he has the height factor against him as well—he's 6'1". He has explosive power at 273 pounds, and is noted for his quickness and overall athletic ability. He clocked 5:00 in the 40.

A native Chicagoan, Chris Zorich of Notre Dame was quoted as saying, "I'd pay to play for the Bears," endearing him forever to the team's finance director. He also endeared himself to Mike Ditka, who said back in February, "If ever there was a kid born to be a Chicago Bear and wear a Chicago Bear uniform, it is Chris Zorich. I really love this kid"—a predraft statement that probably did not endear Ditka to the club's finance director. Winner of the Lombardi Award (for college football's finest lineman), Zorich has the size shortcoming, however: He's 6'1" and 267 pounds. He runs the 40 at 4:75, fastest of all tackles rated by National, and graded out at 6.0.

There are a few other tackles teams will be taking a close look at: Esera Tuaolo of Oregon State (6'2¼", 260 pounds, 4:82 in the 40, graded 6.4), David Rocker of Auburn (6'3", 264 pounds, 4.95 in the 40, graded 6.5), and George Thornton of Alabama (6'3", 293 pounds, 5:10 in the 40, graded 5.6).

Defensive ends are always a sought-after commodity in the NFL draft. In the past, it was often tough to gauge them since their pass-rush ability was never fully exposed to the scouts, simply because there was not a lot of passing in the college game. But today all that is different, with the likes of Miami (Florida), Brigham Young, and Stanford replacing the old grind-it-out-on-the-ground offenses personified by the Ohio State–Michigan games of days gone by. They even pass a lot in the Big Ten today.

Because so many college teams use the 3–4 defense, there are a number of defensive ends who could just as easily be classified as defensive tackles and may very well end up at that position in the NFL.

Lamar Rogers of Auburn is highly touted. He has the size (6'3½" and 276 pounds) and speed (4:86 in the 40) and graded out best according to National, at 7.1. *The National Sports Daily* rates him the sixth best defensive lineman in the 1991 draft. He is considered convertible to a tackle, and a number of teams are considering him as such. The Bears have some reservations about his three Ms, but they are not really concerned, because the general feeling is that he won't be around anyway when it comes to the twenty-second pick.

Next is Huey Richardson of Florida, graded 7.0, who Rod Graves scouted and is prepared to lobby strongly for if he is still around when the Bears choose. Richardson, at 6'5" and 236 pounds, played linebacker his junior year in the 3–4 defense and end his senior year in the 4–3 defense. He turned in the best 40 of all ends rated by National with a 4:66. He is considered a fine pass rusher, and it will be interesting to see what position he is utilized at by the team who drafts him.

Kelvin Pritchett of Mississippi, at 6'3" and 265 pounds, has played at both defensive end and tackle. He is well-regarded by most teams around the league, but National only ranks him as the twelfth most appealing defensive end, grading him 5.7. He runs the 40 in 4:93.

The biggest question mark in this year's draft is the end without credential, Eric Swann (6'4", 310 pounds, 4:90 in the 40, ungraded by National), who chose to go to North Carolina State after being recruited by a number of major colleges but never attended because he was unable to meet the minimum score on the Scholastic Aptitude Test (SATs) required by the NCAA. So instead he played for the semipro Bay City (Massachusetts) Titans. He looked impressive at the National Invitational Camp in February, but despite his size, speed, and quite apparent athletic ability, he is looked upon as a major gamble by most. "He's either going to be a Pro Bowler or he's going to cost a player personnel director his job," one owner (not Michael McCaskey) observed. Bear coach Mike Ditka noted, "He ain't playing the Rochester Ruffians anymore."

Other defensive ends who are being carefully considered in the 1991 draft are: Mike Jones of North Carolina State (6'3¼", 276 pounds, 4:93 in the 40, graded 6.51), considered an excellent pass rusher; Phil Hansen of North Dakota State (6'5", 259 pounds, 4:65 in the 40, graded 5.2—National apparently does not think as much of him as the other analysts), who has the added capability of long-snap centering on punting situations; Robert Young of Mississippi State (6'7", 261 pounds, 4:85 in the 40, graded 5.9); Mel Agee of Illinois (6'5", 288 pounds, 5:09 in the 40, graded 6.9)—that's third best, according to National); Shane Curry of Miami (Florida) (6'5", 253 pounds, 5:03 in the 40, graded 5.1), who can also play defensive tackle, which is what some think he will be drafted as; and Andy Harmon of Kent State (6'4", 255 pounds, 4:71 in the 40, graded 5.51).

*　　*　　*

106

Good linebackers get almost as much press as the glamour boys on the other side of the line of scrimmage (quarterbacks, running backs, wide receivers); one thinks of the legendary names like Bulldog Turner (Chicago Bears), George Connor (Chicago Bears), Chuck Bednarik (Philadelphia Eagles), Bill George (Chicago Bears), Joe Schmidt (Detroit Lions), Sam Huff (New York Giants), Dick Butkus (Chicago Bears), Ray Nitschke (Green Bay Packers), Ted Hendricks (Baltimore Colts), Jack Lambert and Jack Ham (Pittsburgh Steelers), and today's Mike Singletary (Chicago Bears) and Lawrence Taylor (New York Giants). And their compensation is commensurate with their press coverage.

The 1991 crop of linebackers could be considered a decent harvest, especially when those defensive ends who may well turn out to be NFL linebackers are included. The selection could have been spectacular if linebackers like Keith McCants, Junior Seau, and Lamar Lathon had not come out as juniors the year before.

Clearly, one of the most sought after players in 1991 is outside linebacker Mike Croel of Nebraska. Everyone rates him very high, and he is expected to go within the first five picks. Croel stands 6'2½", weighs 226 pounds, runs the 40 in 4:44 (faster than most wide receivers and running backs in this year's draft), and is graded at 7.5. He is equally good at chasing down running backs, covering passes, and blitzing the passer. The Bears are somewhat comfortable with their linebackers and backup linebackers, but they have made it clear they are interested in another one. Whether they are willing to trade up for Croel, however, is questionable.

Croel is a most interesting personality. He is black, but was adopted and raised in a foster home by two white parents. His father, Philip Croel, said, "When we were living outside of Chicago, our neighbors came over and asked what right we had bringing a black child into a white house. . . . Another time, they asked if we would try to keep Michael inside because they wanted to sell their house."

Mike Croel lived in Detroit, Chicago, Boston, Los Altos, California, and finally Lincoln, Nebraska, where he ultimately honed his football skills for the Cornhuskers.

Once, he remembered, "I was in kindergarten and I used to go to this bus stop and wait for my sister. This kid came off the bus and called me 'nigger.' That was *the* worst word. All I knew was that was not the word to call me. I chased him around the neighborhood and got tired and went home." According to the scouts, there are a lot of NFL quarterbacks and running backs who will be running around the neighborhood to get away from Mike Croel.

Besides Croel, there are a few other rather attractive outside linebackers garnering interest from various NFL teams. Alfred Williams of Colorado is considered a probable first-round selection. He checks in at 6'5¼" and 229 pounds, runs the 40 at 4:71, grades 7.0, and is considered one of the very best pass rushers available (he had a school-record 35½ career sacks). On the downside, he is not considered a highly motivated ballplayer and performed poorly at the National Invitational Camp in Indianapolis earlier this year.

Also from Colorado is Kanavis McGhee, who can play either outside linebacker or defensive end. He is 6'3½", 246 pounds, runs the 40 in 4:70, and grades 6.5. Because of his versatility and seemingly greater dedication to the game, some think he may go before teammate Williams.

Other notable outside linebackers are Godfrey Myles of Florida (6'1½", 242 pounds, 4:50 in the 40, graded 6.11); Dixon Edwards of Michigan State (6'1", 222 pounds, 4:60 in the 40, graded 6.0); Roman Phifer of UCLA (6'2", 225 pounds, 4:65 in the 40, graded 6.0); William Thomas of Texas A & M (6'2½", 207 pounds, 4:71 in the 40, graded 5.8); and Carlos Jenkins of Michigan State (6'3½", 212 pounds, 4:65 in the 40, graded 5.51).

The top inside linebacker is considered to be Keith Traylor of the rather obscure Central State (Oklahoma). National graded him at 7.0, and the next closest was only 5.7. Traylor, who is 6'2¼", 253 pounds, and runs the 40 in 4:69, is somewhat of a question mark, both because he seems prone to injuries, missing games in both his junior and senior years, and because of the size of the school he played for and therefore the relative quality of competition he played against.

There are a few other inside linebackers who many speculate may go in the later rounds of the draft: Mike Stonebreaker of Notre Dame (6'0½", 230 pounds, 4:75 in the 40, graded 5.7) Darrick Brownlow of Illinois (5'10¼", 237 pounds, 4:75 in the 40, graded 5.1), and Pat Tyrance of Nebraska (6'1¾", 242 pounds, 4:51 in the 40, graded 5.1).

Defensive backs, so highly visible when they destroy a leaping wide receiver with a thunderous hit or when they are embarrassingly beaten by one for a touchdown, must have eclectic talents. They have to be able not only to survive but to prevail in collisions with 250-pound tight ends or 240-pound fullbacks, race alongside wide receivers of world-class speed, and tackle dazzling running backs in the open field. Good ones are always in great demand.

As Dan Pompei, a staff writer for the *Chicago Sun-Times*, said in assessing the 1991 draft, "The Bears go through cornerbacks like babies go through diapers. As usual, they need some this April." The reason for that need is that they sent one, Vestee Jackson, to Tampa Bay in the trade for defensive end Eric Kumerow, and another, Lemuel Stinson, is coming off serious reconstructive knee surgery and no one can predict a full recovery.

It is a good year for defensive backs, and a number are expected to be first-round choices. Cornerback Todd Lyght of Notre Dame is the only player in the draft to grade 8.0 besides wide receiver Reggie Barrett of Texas–El Paso (8.2), which means National projects him as a sure rookie starter. Many analysts and scouts feel he will go as the second pick in the first round, right after Fighting Irish teammate Rocket Ismail. Lyght, a converted wide receiver, is 6'1", 184 pounds, and runs the 40 in 4:45. Bill Tobin, however, does not rate him as high a cornerback as the Bears did Donnell Woolford, the eleventh pick of the first round in 1989.

The National does not regard Bruce Pickens of Nebraska nearly as high as it does Lyght, 6.01, fifteenth in its list of cornerbacks. Almost nobody else is in agreement. Joel Buchsbaum, pro football guru of *Pro Football Weekly*, rates Pickens just a short step behind Lyght; so does John Czarnecki, who filled the same roll for *The National Sports Daily*. Some around Halas Hall feel that Pickens just might be *the best* cornerback available. Pickens is no giant at 5'11", 191 pounds, but he is fast—4:50 in the 40—and is considered awesome in his pass-coverage skills.

Aeneas Williams of Southern (the one in Louisiana) is National's second highest rated cornerback, at 7.0. He is pretty small—5'10" and 190 pounds—but his 4:38 in the 40 is the swiftest of all twenty-six cornerbacks graded by National. *Pro Football Weekly* suggests he might be better-positioned as a free safety.

Then there is Steve Jackson of Purdue, a chunky, dwarfish 5'8½", 182-pounder who is known for his toughness but can also run the 40 in 4:45 and was graded out by National as the number three cornerback, at 6.7. Following Jackson, at least according to National, is Henry Jones of Illinois. At 5'11¾" and 196 pounds, a 4:50 in the 40, and a grading of 6.61, he is considered a very good prospect because he can fill in either at cornerback or safety. Another highly valued cornerback on the Bears' list is Ohio State's Vince Clark. He is 6'0" and 186 pounds and can run the 40 in 4:39, just a short nose behind Aeneas Williams. He was graded out sixth by National at 6.51.

There are others who will undoubtedly go relatively early in the draft, including Darryl Lewis of Arizona (5'8½", 182 pounds,

4:58 in the 40, graded 6.6); Marcus Robertson of Iowa State (5'11", 193 pounds, 4:50 in the 40, graded 6.5); Jerome Henderson of Clemson (5'11", 188 pounds, 4:42 in the 40, graded 6.31); Dave McCloughan of Colorado (6'0", 184 pounds, 4:65 in the 40, graded 6.3); Joe Johnson of North Carolina State (5'9", 185 pounds, 4:48 in the 40, graded 6.2); and the minuscule Kevin Scott of Stanford (5'9", 168 pounds, 4:42 in the 40, graded only 5.3 but considered by many a true sleeper).

There are also a handful of juniors who have come out and are especially liked by the pros. Foremost is Dexter Davis from Clemson, rather small at 5'9" and 175 pounds, but with 4:62 in the 40 and high marks on intensity of play. And there is also Sammy Walker (5'11", 192 pounds, 4:60 in the 40) of Texas Tech.

And Joel Buchsbaum of *Pro Football Weekly* says Darryl Wren (6'0", 186 pounds, 4:55 in the 40) of Pittsburgh (Kansas) State is a *true* sleeper.

At safety, where the Bears have recent memories of hitmen like Doug Plank, Gary Fencik, and Dave Duerson, the feeling is not one of nostalgia. The powers in Halas Hall are quite content with their previous year's first-round draft choice, Mark Carrier at free safety, and veteran Shaun Gayle at strong safety, plus their respective backups, Markus Paul and David Tate. But there are some good safety prospects in this year's draft.

Highest on the National's list is Mike Dumas of Indiana; highest on most other lists is Eric Turner of UCLA.

Eric Turner has all the requisites—size, strength, power, speed, natural athletic instinct; that's why so many scouts like him. Don King, who scouted him for the Bears, would love to see him in the blue and orange, but feels there is no way he will still be around when the Bears draft. Turner is 6'1" and 207 pounds, with 4.68 speed in the 40, and can and will hit with joyful explosiveness. National gives him a grade of 6.5. Scouts say he has a definite future in the NFL and maybe one in the Pro Bowl.

Dumas, who graded out at 6.6, is not really a Mack-truck hitter, because he is only 5'11" and 175 pounds. But he has excellent speed—4:50 in the 40—and, according to the Bears' scouting reports, has great instinctual abilities for the position.

Another well-regarded safety is Stanley Richard of Texas. Jim Parmer scouted him and sings a song of praise, although National thinks he is only worthy of a ranking of fifth at the safety position, grading him 6.2. But he is swift (4:50 in the 40) and, according to Parmer, is lean and mean at 6'1½" and 197 pounds. *The National Sports Daily* rates him as the fifth most attractive defensive back in this year's draft. *Sport* magazine has him third.

One of the other most highly rated safeties is a junior, Jesse Campbell of North Carolina State, who many believe will go in the second or third round. He is a strong, aggressive defensive back at 6'2" and 212 pounds, and fast, with a 4:55 clocking in the 40; he could also play cornerback in the NFL. A lot of teams are looking at him.

There is also Merton Hanks of Iowa (6'1½", 184 pounds, 4:60 in the 40, graded 6.0). But that is about it for safety, unless there is a sleeper out there.

Last on the Bears' war room wall, and last on the rest of the teams' walls, too, are the kickers—placekickers and punters—even though they can make an incredible difference in the outcome of a game. Only a handful in the fifty-five years of the draft have been taken in the first round—punter Ray Guy by Oakland in 1973; placekicker Steve Little by St. Louis in 1978; placekicker Russell Erxleben in 1979 by New Orleans; and placekicker Tony Zendejas by the Redskins in the 1984 supplemental draft.

None are expected to go in the first round of the 1991 draft.

The Bears are interested, in a coy sort of way. In Kevin Butler, they have one of the most consistent placekickers in the game.

But he has had trouble getting kickoffs down the field to a depth that the Bears want. And there have been problems with their punting game under the foot of Maury Buford, who has in the last year or two left something to be desired. So they are looking around.

The most appealing appears to be Chris Gardocki of Clemson. A junior, and therefore unranked by National, he is a left-footed kicker who both placekicks and punts. In fact, he is only the second player in NCAA history to rank in the top five in both field-goal kicking and punting in the same year. If he could perform both functions in the NFL, he could save a roster spot on the team that takes him.

National rates the placekickers in this order: Robbie Keen of California (5.0), Mike Pollack of Texas (4.8), Jeff Shudak of Iowa State (4.6), John Kasay of Georgia (4.5), and Ed Beaulac of California/Sonoma (4.4).

Punters rate in this order: Brian Greenfield of Pittsburgh (6.0), Paul Alsbury of Southwest Texas (4.8), Greg Hertzog of West Virginia (4.6), Jeff Fite of Memphis State (4.41), and Eric Nyhus of Washington (Missouri) (4.4).

There seems to be neither a Lou Groza, George Blanda, Jan Stenerud, Jim Bakken, or Pat Leahy, nor a Sammy Baugh, Horace Gillom, Yale Lary, or Ray Guy in this draft.

But then . . . one never knows . . . not in the meat market.

THE
WEEK BEFORE

The week before the draft, the suspense builds daily—mostly for the 600 or so college seniors and juniors who feel they have a legitimate shot at being drafted. Of those 600, there are maybe 150 to 200 who can feel truly confident they will be drafted, and the suspense for them is in terms of what round they will be taken. There are just a handful who are considered cinches to go in the first round.

It is a long and difficult road from the college football playing field to that of the NFL. Think of it this way. There are 196 colleges in NCAA Division 1-A and 1-AA with major football programs, all of which are religiously scouted by the pros and the scouting combines. Each team has perhaps twenty-five certified starters—offense, defense, and specialty players like placekickers, punters, and kick returners. That turns out to be 4,900 college players who are looked at in a given year.

Of the 4,900, only about 400 or so will be invited to the National Invitational Camp at the Hoosier Dome in Indianapolis for close scrutiny by NFL teams. And only 336 will actually be drafted.

And a college player's worries are far from over even after he has been afforded the luxury of being selected in one of the twelve rounds of the draft. Less than half of those drafted will ever play in an NFL regular-season game. In the 1990s, it is estimated that a total of approximately 140 to 150 draftees, or rookie free agents, will make the opening day rosters of NFL teams.

In sum, that is about 3 percent of the 4,900 college starters who could conceivably harbor dreams of making it to the pros. The NFL is an exclusive club.

There is suspense for the fans, too, generated by the media the week before the draft. The upcoming draft is widely covered in newspapers and on radio and television. The college prospects are assessed, NFL team needs are debated, related events and trades are reported, speculations fly.

There is little suspense in the team war rooms, however. There, the work has already been done. Sure, there are trade plots and trade talks, and discussions of who the team will take if more than one of its premier wish-list players is available when its turn comes. But for the most part, the strategies are in place and await adaptation as the draft scenario unfolds on D-Day.

At the start of the week before the draft, the Bears pretty well have their program in order. They are prepared for D-Day. The players at all positions have been discussed by the scouts and Bill Tobin. Tobin has given them their final Bear grade. The Bear priorities have been discussed with Mike Ditka and Michael Mc-Caskey. They are all well understood by the Bear triumvirate, who make the final decision, and the scouts, who have been talking up their players for the previous two weeks: offensive line, defensive line, a speedy wide receiver . . . down the line a defensive back and probably a quarterback. And what the members of the media do not know, and do not even conjecture is that the Bears are talking, talking seriously, about a kicker.

The lists of players and grades are not on the war room wall yet. They will not be put there until just before the draft itself. For security purposes, they remain under the guard of Bill Tobin.

Each of the scouts has his own particular hopes of who might be there in the first couple of rounds, the ones he has scouted and is high on, looking on them almost like his own personal protégés. To a man, the Bear powers and scouts would like to see the two enormous tackles from Tennessee there—Antone Davis and Charles McRae—or defensive tackle Russell Maryland of Miami (Florida), who impressed them all so much at the National Invitational Camp back in February, or Notre Dame cornerback Todd Lyght, but realistically they are also quite certain those players will have been long gone by the time the twenty-second selection comes up.

There are others, though, who just might still be there. Rod Graves would like the opportunity to lobby for defensive end or possible linebacker Huey Richardson of Florida; Don King has some hope that tackle Pat Harlow of Southern Cal or wide receiver Mike Pritchard of Colorado might still be there for harvesting; Jim Parmer has his fingers crossed that Texas tackle Stan Thomas will still be available. And they have other favorites for the later rounds.

Much of this buildup week, however, is spent discussing the needs and priorities of the other NFL teams and conducting mock drafts. In this way, the Bears can get a feel for the eventualities. For this they rely a lot on local newspapers from other NFL cities and the trade journals, like *Pro Football Weekly* and *The National Sports Daily*. Ken Geiger, the Bears' pro scout, is also a major source of information about the needs and desires of the other teams in the NFL.

"During this last week," Rod Graves explains, "we try to guesstimate what the needs are of the other teams that will go before us. That's our process of mock drafting; it's a verbal one between the scouts and Bill [Tobin]." He adds, however: "Since

I've been there the draft has never fallen as we thought it would. There are always surprises.''

Jim Parmer, who has been at it with the Bears for almost two decades, corroborates this: ''Mock drafting? If you're picking fifth or sixth you could possibly accurately determine who is going to be there. On twenty-second, though, it's really hard to determine, because there are always so many surprises in the first round. We try to get the best and the worst scenario. It does help a lot, though, to assess what the other teams need or want, and we spend a good amount of time doing that the week before the draft.''

''You do your best to get ready, get everything in place,'' Bill Tobin says, ''and you hope it's going to turn out to be one of those super draft years.'' And the Bears have had more than a couple of them: Of what are generally considered the six best drafts ever, the Bears own three.

First there was the 1940 draft, when the Bears picked up future Hall of Famers center Bulldog Turner and halfback George Mc-Afee, as well as such stalwarts as end Ken Kavanaugh, halfback Scooter McLean, tackle Lee Artoe, and halfback Harry Clark.

Then there was the 1965 draft, when Chicago selected another pair of Hall of Famers, running back Gale Sayers and linebacker Dick Butkus. They also profited by the selection of wide receiver Dick Gordon. Two others the Bears picked that year went on to have fine careers in the AFL, defensive end Steve DeLong with the San Diego Chargers and fullback Jim Nance with the Boston/ New England Patriots.

Three of the other four exceptional drafts were turned in by the Green Bay Packers, the Pittsburgh Steelers, and the Dallas Cowboys. In 1958, Green Bay got two future Hall of Famers, linebacker Ray Nitschke and fullback Jim Taylor, as well as guard Jerry Kramer and center Dan Currie. In 1974, the Steelers took Hall of Fame middle linebacker Jack Lambert, wide receivers

Lynn Swann and John Stallworth, and center Mike Webster. And in 1975, Dallas signed defensive tackle Randy White, linebacker Thomas "Hollywood" Henderson, linebacker Bob Bruenig, guard Herbert Scott, running back Scott Laidlaw, and guard Burton Lawless.

The Bears' third great draft year was also 1975, the first year the present-day president of the New Orleans Saints, Jim Finks, was drafting for them. That year they took in the first round Walter Payton, who was destined to become the NFL's all-time leading ground gainer (16,726 yards rushing over a thirteen-year career), as well as a bevy of future starters: fullback Roland Harper, quarterback Bob Avellini, defensive end Mike Hartenstine, safety Doug Plank, guard Revie Sorey, and cornerback Virgil Livers.

But that is all history. It is *now* that Bill Tobin and his crew of scouts have to think about. And so they get down to it at Halas Hall.

In 1991, the Dallas Cowboys have three choices in the first round—their own and one each from Minnesota and New Orleans, pick numbers 11, 12, and 14. Because that gives them strong bargaining power, there is a lot of speculation they might trade up or down.

Rumors now are everywhere that the New England Patriots would like to unload the number one pick if the deal is right. The Bears are not interested in it, and Bill Tobin told the Patriots that a few weeks earlier. But does someone else want the Rocket, with his platinum price tag? Jim Parmer has heard there is interest down his way, Texas, from both the Houston Oilers and the Dallas Cowboys. Then there are the Washington Redskins, whose owner, Jack Kent Cooke, is not at all hesitant about throwing the dollars around (and where great receiver Art Monk is in his mid-thirties). And San Francisco 49ers' owner, Eddie DeBartolo, Jr., is also very generous—he has *two* quarterbacks who earn more than $2 million a year (Joe Montana and Steve Young). The Atlanta Falcons, it is said, may be interested as well, although they already have a lot of pizzazz down there in Georgia with the effervescent "Neon" Deion Sanders playing cornerback for them.

If New England does not trade its pick, the unanimous feeling is that it will go for the glitter and take Rocket Ismail, even though wide receiver is one of the positions at which the team is least hurting; it is weakest in the offensive line and the defensive backfield. The mock drafts at Halas Hall are conducted with two scenarios, the Rocket going to New England and the Rocket going to a team that traded up for him.

It is generally believed that the Patriots want one or two instant starters, somebody like cornerback Todd Lyght of Notre Dame or safety Eric Turner of UCLA or one of the Tennessee tackles, Antone Davis and Charles McRae. Joe Mendes, their director of player operations, has also let it be known to the press that they are seriously looking at this year's crop of running backs. Coming off a 1–15–0 season, they need help in a lot of places. With the first pick in each of the twelve rounds of the draft and three additional selections in the fourth round, however, they stand a good chance of filling some of their more pressing needs. *Mock Draft: Raghib Ismail, WR, Notre Dame.*

The Cleveland Browns have the second choice, and it is generally conceded they will keep it. They are in need of a quality cornerback, and Todd Lyght should be there for the reaping. With Rocket going on the first pick, Lyght's name keeps popping up in the mock drafts as number two in '91. But the Browns, too, have definite needs in their offensive line, and names like Antone Davis, Charles McRae, and Pat Harlow slip in from time to time. Bill Tobin wonders if they really will take a defensive back with the second pick, given all the other prime meat available.

Owner Art Modell and general manager Ernie Accorsi will be

making the decisions this draft with little input from new coach Bill Belichick, who is just starting his first year as pilot of the Browns. Accorsi has said he is also interested in wide receivers, but the Rocket is not one of them. Tight end is another consideration, the scouts bring up, now that the longtime stalwart at that position for the Browns, Ozzie Newsome, has just retired. But there is not a certified first-rounder to be found. Later, the Browns might like some help in the defensive line and at wide receiver. *Mock Draft: Todd Lyght, CB, Notre Dame.*

The Atlanta Falcons have a problem, but it's one most teams in the NFL would like to have. They have the third pick in the draft as well as the thirteenth (which they received the year before when they traded the first pick to Indianapolis so the Colts could take the quarterback they so much wanted, Illinois's Jeff George). The problem is, Who do you take third and who do you take ten picks down the line? Having two such high selections does not make a player personnel director's life all that easy, as Bill Tobin points out, because the one you take third might have still been there at number 13, while the one you were hoping for at 13 might be gone when you get there.

With two first-round choices like this, you are dealing with a very good hand if you want to trade up and take Rocket Ismail. And there are rumors to that effect. On the other hand, as Rod Graves points out, that might not be a big priority because the Falcons have a blazer of a wide receiver, Andre Rison, whom they acquired the year before and who played outstandingly enough to go to the Pro Bowl from a team that won only five of its sixteen games. But then, with Rison *and* the Rocket racing downfield at the same time . . . The question is, Do they have a quarterback to get the ball to them? Outspoken coach Jerry Glanville has made it clear he would like a quarterback in the 1991 draft, especially with Atlanta's starter, Chris Miller, carrying a bunch of pins in his shoulder after an injury in 1990.

Personnel director Ken Herock, word has it around Halas Hall, is looking for a cornerback, and there are a couple of very good ones out there this year. And Herock has the final say down in Atlanta. The Falcons also might go for linebacker Mike Croel of Nebraska, who seems far and away the best at that position, which is another of Atlanta's top priorities, and he most likely will not be there when the thirteenth pick is called.

The Bears feel reasonably comfortable that the Falcons, their priorities and options being what they are, will not snatch one of those players at the top of the wish-list of Tobin/Ditka/McCaskey.

Deeper in the draft, Atlanta may also want some help on its defensive line. *Mock Draft: Mike Croel, LB, Nebraska.*

The Denver Broncos, however, might very well beat the Bears to the punch. According to what is being written in the *Denver Post* sports pages, they are definitely in the market for an offensive tackle. *Chicago Tribune* sportswriter Don Pierson says in a predraft analysis: "With [their two offensive tackles] Ken Lanier getting old and Gerald Perry getting arrested [he has had his off-field problems], offensive tackle is a definite need." And there will certainly be several of the four outstanding ones available when the fourth pick comes up. That's what the outside observers are saying; inside, one hears different.

The Broncos have a variety of needs. They need a good pass-rushing outside linebacker, and that brings Mike Croel to mind, if he has not already been gobbled up, or maybe even Huey Richardson of Florida. Coach Dan Reeves is the power play here when it comes to the final decision, one of the few coaches who really is, and he is very tight-mouthed around draft time. At the same time, his pal and former coaching-mate down at the Dallas Cowboys in the 1970s, Mike Ditka, has said Reeves really wants Mike Croel. The talk among the Bears is that if Croel is not available, the Broncos may even choose to move down in the draft. After all, the fourth pick is going to cost you megabucks, and if the guy you (Dan Reeves) really want is not there . . . well.

121

Defensive backs are another consideration, both at corner and safety, and there will be some nice pickings there as well. Denver has a lot of ways it can go, and one or two of them could affect the Bears eighteen picks down the ladder.

Defense may be the priority in the later rounds. *Mock Draft: Antone Davis, OT, Tennessee.*

Drafting fifth, the Los Angeles Rams need help in a lot of places, especially their defensive line. It is a known fact that coach John Robinson would love to have Russell Maryland if the big, swift defensive tackle is still around. The Bears think he might be; so do a lot of the analysts who conduct their own personal mock drafts the week before D-Day. If he is not, there is Bobby Wilson of Michigan State, also interesting to John Robinson. The talk is that the ordinarily conservative Rams would not want to take a chance, at least in the first round, on either the college-less Eric Swann or controversial Ted Washington of Louisville.

On the other hand, their offensive tackles are older by several years than those of the Bears, and age is an overriding concern with the Bears, so it must be with the Rams as well. Pat Harlow played that position exceptionally well in 1990 just up the road from the Rams at Southern Cal, where John Robinson coached for a decade during the late 1970s and early '80s. Maybe they will opt for a hometown boy.

There is speculation that Robinson likes running backs Nick Bell of Iowa and Leonard Russell of Arizona State, both big, bruising runners; in the lower draft slots, defensive linemen and linebackers, perhaps.

Like the Bears, the Rams' final decision is made by a triumvirate: Robinson, vice president John Shaw, and personnel director John Math. The mock drafters feel that what they will do with the fifth pick could go any of several ways. *Mock Draft: Russell Maryland, DT, Miami (Florida).*

The Phoenix Cardinals follow the Rams. And like the Rams,

they have a lot of holes to fill—most pressingly, it seems, on the defensive line and in the defensive backfield.

Despite that, second-year head coach Joe Bugel, who had been the offensive line coach for the Washington Redskins before coming to Phoenix, has expressed more than a passing interest in either of the Tennessee tackles, Antone Davis or Charles McRae, and was quoted as saying, "One of those big boys might be around, and I think if one was we'd have to give him a long look."

Most draft decisions in the Cardinal organization, however, are ultimately made by general manager Larry Wilson and player personnel director George Boone—owner Bill Bidwill has a lot of input as well—and nobody has a clear notion of the direction of the team's thinking.

Almost unanimously, the outside mock drafters think the Cardinals will go with one of the Tennessee twosome. But if defensive tackle Russell Maryland is still around that could change their thinking rather quickly. There are also a number of fine defensive backs who should be available, but the feeling is that Phoenix will wait a few rounds before addressing its defensive-backfield needs.

The concern expressed by some at the Bears is that if the Cardinals do take one of the major offensive linemen, it will just add to the possibility that one of the several Chicago might want will not be there when its turn is finally called.

Farther down, the Cardinals seem most interested in defensive players, linemen, and the secondary. *Mock Draft: Charles McRae, OT, Tennessee.*

The Tampa Bay Buccaneers, who own the seventh pick in the first round, do not have a great reputation for successful drafting. As J. David Miller, a contributing editor to *Sport* magazine, observed in an article before the 1991 NFL draft, "If bad decisions had a museum, [Tampa Bay owner] Hugh Culverhouse would be the curator." He was referring most directly to the selection of quarterback Vinny Testaverde, the very pricey first, and ultimately disappointing, pick of the 1987 draft, who, if there were a concert hall for boos and hisses in Tampa, would be the maestro at the podium. As Miller put it, "Vinny Testaverde might be colorblind [which he is], but he couldn't play if he *could* see." *Chicago Tribune* analyst and writer Don Pierson offers a similar observation: "The Bucs need to get a life. They get less out of more high picks than any other team."

So that's where the Buccaneers begin in '91. Who knows, maybe their luck will change.

Because Tampa Bay plays in the NFC Central and therefore meets the Bears twice each year, the group at Halas Hall has a pretty good idea of what the Bucs' needs are. They start off with offensive guard, offensive tackle, a safety, a wide receiver, and a running back. The first two are not happy priorities to the Bears' way of thinking, in terms of their own priorities. Scout Jim Parmer has expressed concern because the offensive lineman he regards so highly, Stan Thomas of Texas, can play *either* tackle or guard, but his worry is somewhat assuaged by the fact that this early in the draft there will undoubtedly be several of the top four or five offensive linemen available to the Bucs. And Parmer does not think they know fellow-Texan Thomas like *he* knows Thomas.

It is thought the Bucs might go for Pat Harlow of Southern Cal if Antone Davis and Charles McRae have already been taken, or perhaps safety Eric Turner of UCLA.

One Bear observer mentions that Tampa Bay ought to make this one a helluva good choice, because it does not have its first-rounder in 1992, which will probably be a high one since Tampa Bay, at least in the Bears' estimation, runs a good shot at ending up at the bottom of the NFC Central Division. (The Bucs traded their 1992 first-rounder to the Indianapolis Colts so they could obtain a quarterback to back up the questionable Testaverde, Chris Chandler.) *Mock Draft: Eric Turner, S, UCLA.*

The Green Bay Packers are a struggling team, too. They have

their own form of Vinny Testaverde: They drafted the so-called combination Arnold Schwarzenegger/Robocop of offensive linemen, Tony Mandarich, with the second pick of the 1989 draft, made him the richest offensive lineman in NFL history, and then found out he could not pass-block. The next year they had two number ones, running back Darrell Thompson and linebacker Tony Bennett, neither of whom saw any notable action for the green and gold.

The Packers definitely need some help in protecting their gilded quarterback Don Majkowski, the highest-paid Packer in franchise history, who, before he was injured the year before, could only have been more in harm's way had he been in the ring with Mike Tyson or trying to dance his way across a Los Angeles freeway.

Word is, however, that the Packers are looking for a defensive lineman. But they will have to stretch to find one worthy of such an early first-round choice, unless by chance Russell Maryland is ignored by teams drafting earlier, which is unlikely. A Bobby Wilson of Michigan State, on the other hand, might not be too long a stretch, and it is likely he will be around. A running back who can, say, gain some yards on the ground (the year before, their top rusher gained 311 yards) is a possibility, too, but this is another area of the draft that is less than impressive. Coach Lindy Infante, it is said, would like a Mack-truck runner like Nick Bell of Iowa.

One Green Bay scout said to the press, however, "We need a fast back who can break one, like Harvey Williams [the running back from Louisiana State who is expected to go in the first round], and a corner, maybe a Bruce Pickens [Nebraska] or Vince Clark [Ohio State], who might still be around [when the Pack drafts eighth]." There does not seem to be a lot of synchronized thinking going on in the land of cheese and bratwurst.

But it is general manager Tom Braatz who makes the final decision here, despite the fact that he has not been on the best of drafting streaks.

The Bears think the Packers will take a defensive back or a defensive lineman. After all, in the three preceding drafts the Packers have taken a running back early, none of whom have worked out, and Tom Braatz may be feeling a little uneasy at this player position. One Bear scout said, "My God, one of these years they gotta come up with a good first-rounder. When was the last one? [James] Lofton [wide receiver, 1978]?" It has been a long time.

Linebackers and running backs will be high on the Green Bay wish-list later on in the draft. *Mock Draft: Bobby Wilson, DT, Michigan State.*

Following Green Bay are the San Diego Chargers with the ninth pick. What this AFL team has is what the NFL Washington Redskins used to have—general manager Bobby Beathard, one of the best of the wheeler-dealers in the game, in the same Hall of Fame league in this area as Gil Brandt of the Cowboys of yesteryear and Jim Finks of the Minnesota Vikings/Chicago Bears/ New Orleans Saints. All three team-builders, through their manipulations and acuity, have brought their teams to various Super Bowls.

Beathard is not, obviously, dependent on first-round draft choices—the Redskins he left are experiencing their first first-round draft pick since 1983—but he knows how to get players who perform. He is on the telephone about the same amount of time as Bill Tobin is out there on the road looking at prospects. There is serious talk he will trade away his first-round pick in 1991 for a deal that will enable him to start putting together a well-rounded San Diego team that will get back in the running in the AFC West.

On the other hand, Beathard—and he does call the signals in the San Diego war room—according to *The National Sports Daily*, "loves Antone Davis . . . and might trade up to get him." Maybe, a good number of people think, he will simply settle for his ninth pick this year, a lean year, because there might not be all that much worthwhile talent in the ensuing rounds.

The talk among the Bears is that if he keeps his pick, it will be either an offensive lineman, perhaps McRae, Harlow, or Thomas if Davis is not around; or a safety, Eric Turner and Stanley Richard being the top prospects here.

It's guys like Bobby Beathard who can mess up many a mock draft. *Mock Draft: Beathard will trade; if not—Stanley Richard, S, Texas.*

Next up are the Detroit Lions, whose run-and-shoot offense is well-staffed in the backfield with Barry Sanders (Heisman Trophy winner and first-round selection two years earlier), who led the NFL in rushing yardage in 1990, and quarterback Rodney Peete, although he is injury-prone and although Andre Ware, his backup, has, to be diplomatic, not lived up to expectations. J. David Miller of *Sport* magazine, who tends not to be diplomatic, quotes an unidentified AFC scout regarding Ware: "He's a bad player. Iraqi SCUDs are more accurate. When he lets it go, you have no idea where it's going."

Coach Wayne Fontes has been making the draft decisions, but after two consecutive losing seasons (7–9–0 in 1989 and 6–10–0 in 1990), there is talk he will be getting some front office advice this year.

The priority here, it is generally agreed, would be a top-flight wide receiver. The Rocket will not be there, but three or four others should be; rumor has it that Fontes likes Herman Moore of Virginia. But the Lions also need a good pass-rushing defensive lineman, maybe a Huey Richardson of Florida. Both should be available when theirs, the tenth, pick comes up.

After their first pick, the Lions will probably take whoever they think is the best athlete available; at least that is the word among the speculators at Halas Hall. *Mock Draft: Herman Moore, WR, Virginia.*

The Dallas Cowboys control three of the next four selections (eleventh, twelfth, and fourteenth). They could really beef up the onetime but now-faded "America's Team" with three highly regarded players here; still, three first-round contract salaries and signing bonuses might make even the Sultan of Brunei wince. So there is a good deal of conversation as to just how they might trade around.

A distinct possibility is that they would trade up with New England so as to snare the Rocket with the draft's first choice; everyone in the NFL knows that owner Jerry Jones has been and still is in deep discussion with the reigning powers of the Patriots. But there are also future first-round draft choices to trade for along with, say, a second-rounder in 1991. Or perhaps they'll go for an established veteran and a later-round selection or selections. The possibilities are many.

Now guiding the draft-picking in Dallas, since Gil Brandt left along with the rest of the ruling body of the Clint Murchison/Tex Schramm/Tom Landry era–Cowboys, is coach Jimmy Johnson, aided by director of player personnel Bob Ackles and head of scouting Dick Mansperger. Most believe that owner Jerry Jones has more than a finger in the final decision, although he claims he stays out of the drafting process, if not the trading game.

If the Cowboys decide to stay with their three top-round choices, it is believed they will be spent on a defensive tackle, currently their weakest point (maybe a Bobby Wilson or Ted Washington), an offensive lineman (should a top one be left), and either a cornerback or a linebacker. Later on in the draft—and they have two additional choices in the third round and another in the fourth, as well as their own second-rounder (the forty-first pick in the draft)—they will be looking for more beef in both front lines and probably a backup quarterback for Troy Aikman, according to the sportswriters and draft analysts at the *Dallas Morning News.*

Mock Draft: They will trade. If they do not—eleventh, Ted Washington, DT, Louisville; twelfth, Pat Harlow, OT, Southern Cal; fourteenth, Mike Pritchard, WR, Colorado.

Everyone is just sitting around waiting to see what Dallas will do; it may very well have a dramatic effect on the 1991 draft.

Scrunched in among the Cowboys' three picks is the thirteenth, which is also the Atlanta Falcons' second of this year's draft. *Mock Draft: Bruce Pickens, CB, Nebraska.*

The team following the multipick Cowboys and Falcons is Pittsburgh, with the fifteenth selection. Everybody is predicting the Steelers will try to grab a wide receiver to complement Pro Bowler Louis Lipps, who seems to be double-teamed even when he is trotting off the field. The complement could be Herman Moore of Virginia, Mike Pritchard of Colorado, Randal Hill of Miami (Florida), or Alvin Harper of Tennessee. One of them should still be around.

Coach Chuck Noll and player personnel chief Dick Haley, it is reported, are also hunting for a good linebacker; but unless Mike Croel, through some stroke of fate, is still around, there does not seem to be a linebacker worth this fifteenth choice. The Bears are also a little wary that Pittsburgh just might go for an offensive lineman, depending on who is left at the time of its selection—if the fleet of fast receivers has been depleted, a hulk to block for the light-footed Lipps, and whoever is throwing to him might be the choice.

A defensive back is something the Steelers might want later—but not now. *Mock Draft: Alvin Harper, WR, Tennessee.*

The Seattle Seahawks are also in need of a wide receiver, and there have been suggestions that they might try to trade up ahead of Pittsburgh if the receiver they want is still there when the Steelers pick.

At the same time, general manager Tom Flores has been quoted as not ruling out a quarterback in the first round. He and coach Chuck Knox are the ones who will decide this. To those at Halas Hall and among the free-lance analysts, it would not be surprising if Seattle took the first quarterback of the 1991 draft, probably either Dan McGwire of San Diego State or Brett Favre of Mississippi (the unrestrained Todd Marinovich of USC does not fit into the restrained Seahawk approach to the game of professional football).

Wide receiver, if the Seahawks do not take one in the first round, and defensive lineman are priorities after the initial pick. *Mock Draft: Dan McGwire, QB, San Diego State.*

The Houston Oilers, selecting seventeenth, are definitely interested in a defensive back, either corner or safety. Their offense is fine, predominantly based on their freewheeling, rifle-armed quarterback Warren Moon, behind who in 1990 they scored the second-most points in the entire NFL (404, trailing only the Super Bowl–bound Buffalo Bills, who tallied 428).

Houston also has its eye on offensive linemen. Mike Holovak, their general manager, has publicly expressed that he thinks this is one of the worst drafts in the last two decades and may decide to trade down—and he is one of the better-known traders in the NFL.

If defensive backs Todd Lyght, Eric Turner, Stanley Richard, or Bruce Pickens are not around, it would not be surprising, according to Bear sources, to see Holovak trade down and bulk up his team in later rounds. The same is true of offensive linemen, but it is believed that the one or two who Houston would consider will be gone and that therefore this priority will slip to later rounds.

Houston has its eyes on wide receivers, but they are not as brightly focused there as they are on defensive backs, and the Oilers are looking at the former as secondary picks. *Mock Draft: Vince Clark, CB, Ohio State.*

The Cincinnati Bengals, drafting next, are also in need of defensive help. They had a good year in 1990, winning the AFC Central Division, but they gave up a lot of points at the same time (352, a hefty seventy-two more than the next division crown-holder in the NFL, the Chicago Bears, who yielded 280).

A defensive lineman or linebacker heads the list of general

manager Mike Brown, who just so happens to be the son of Hall of Famer Paul Brown, and who also just so happens to be the power broker as far as drafts in Cincinnati are concerned. Unfortunately for Cincinnati, these are two of the less-promising positions in this year's draft. The worthy first-rounders may be gone at these two positions by the time the eighteenth pick comes up, and what might be left are merely second- or third-rounders—at least that is a surmise being kicked around. And it is not good business to draft a second- or third-round choice midway through the first round. So if the certified first-rounder is not there, what will the Bengals do? Maybe draft a running back: it is rumored they like Leonard Russell of Arizona State, who could still be available. As an alternative, they could trade down—and many believe they will.

Other teams and a number of outside analysts think the Bengals have a lot more holes to be filled than those in the Cincinnati war room do. They are, however, a cautious, conservative franchise, and it is commonly believed they will just wait to see if Leonard Russell is there, and, if he's not, take the best defensive player available. They will be all over the field in the later rounds. *Mock Draft: Leonard Russell, RB, Arizona State.*

The Philadelphia Eagles in 1991 finally have the opportunity to be the genuine pain in the ass to the Bears that their former head coach, Buddy Ryan, always wanted them to be. This had been his ultimate wish ever since he left Chicago after serving as defensive coordinator under Mike Ditka for the team that became champions of Super Bowl XX. A constant verbal combatant with Ditka, Ryan was never able to wreak vengeance while he was coaching, his Eagles consistently coming up on the losing end when the two teams met, including the famous "Fog Bowl" playoff game of 1988 at Soldier Field.

Now, with Ryan gone, the Eagles can do it to the Bears. They have announced that they want, above all, a major offensive lineman in this year's draft. Given how many other teams seem to want the same thing, the Eagles may just put the Bears out of the field when their pick, the nineteenth, comes up. Head coach Rich Kotite, who replaced the fired Buddy Ryan, says they want perhaps *three* offensive linemen in the early part of the 1991 draft (he truly wants to protect his scrambling quarterback and franchise-maker, Randall Cunningham). And it is an accepted fact that coach Kotite is running the draft in Philadelphia.

This could be Buddy Ryan's posthumous revenge (figuratively speaking, that is—only Ryan's coaching career is dead).

Kotite has expressed interest in offensive linemen Pat Harlow and Stan Thomas, as well as Ed King of Auburn and Eric Moten of Michigan State, all four of whom might be around when the Eagles draft, he believes. He also has said a running back would not be out of the question.

Harry Gamble, Philadelphia's general manager, also has a say in the matter, and he is known to live up to his name. He has said a trade up is not at all out of the question. In the Bear war room on D-Day, a lot may depend on what Philadelphia decides to do.

Other wishes for the Eagles later on are defensive linemen and running backs. *Mock Draft: Stan Thomas, DT, Texas.*

The Washington Redskins are not used to a draft pick in the first round. It goes all the way back to George "The future is now!" Allen, who coached them and served as general manager from 1971 through 1977. Allen had little care for the draft and instead traded away almost every choice he had to get seasoned veterans, who became known as the "Over-the-Hill Gang."

Bobby Beathard, who took over as general manager in 1978 and stayed around for more than a decade, eventually took up Allen's philosophy—he traded and traded and culled from the lower levels of the draft. Which is why the Redskins did not have a first-round draft choice between 1983 and 1991. However, during his tenure of rebuilding the team, the Redskins went to three Super Bowls (XVII, XVIII, and XXII), winning the first and third of them.

Now Washington again has the opportunity to draft in the first round. Charley Casserly has replaced Beathard as general manager and inherited the ultimate draft duties, although coach Joe Gibbs has a major input.

The admitted priority is defense; a pass rusher and a flashy defensive back seem to be the two people they are looking for. Casserly has also implied he does not want to carry on the tradition of trading away draft choices—"The future is the future," anyone?

The Redskins have evinced interest in defensive tackle Ted Washington, feeling Joe Gibbs will be able to motivate him, but they also like Bobby Wilson and Huey Richardson. If none of them are available, the thought is they will go for the best remaining defensive back.

Washington would like to possess a sampling of defensive backs, so it may look for them in the later rounds. And maybe a running back. *Mock Draft: Huey Richardson, DE/LB, Florida.*

The Kansas City Chiefs have to take into consideration that their quarterback, Steve DeBerg, although still playing well, is thirty-seven years old, and that there is doubt about his existing backups. So a quarterback like Dan McGwire, Todd Marinovich, or Brett Favre, all three projected as possible first-round picks, might just be the man for them.

Coach Marty Schottenheimer is said to want a wide receiver to take the pressure off the first-rate one they already have, Stephone Paige. There are four or five good ones, so there should be one around when Kansas City drafts number 21. The final decision is not rendered by Schottenheimer, but by general manager Carl Peterson, after culling the various opinions of the coach, player personnel director, and scouts.

The Chiefs are also in need of a defensive back and a linebacker, but it is believed that these are not first-round considerations. *Mock Draft: Brett Favre, QB, Southern Mississippi.*

The Bears. We already know their priorities. In the words of

Bill Tobin, "I think the drafts fit us real well. What Mike [Ditka] described as his wish-list—and actually my wish-list, too—is offensive linemen and defensive linemen. There's some quality offensive linemen with some depth. In my opinion that's the strongest area of the draft. I don't want to go into specifics, whether they're center, guards, or tackles. . . . There's been a lot of people [offensive linemen] change positions once they get into the pro game.

"Defensive line. There are some good, solid players. A few of them may not be as tall as you quite like or may not be as fast as you quite like. We don't see a lot of pure 4–3 teams in college football, so very often you're grading linebackers that do some dropping [in pass coverage] and some rushing and [we are] projecting them to defensive ends for our league. There are some decent defensive linemen that we would consider . . . ends and tackles [in the first round].

"There's also a lot of depth in receivers . . . you get an opportunity to see so many receivers now in college. You might be able to get a receiver in the fifth round that's as good as somebody taken in the first or second round or third round.

"I don't see us taking a quarterback in the first round. With our five running backs, I couldn't see us taking an offensive back. I don't know that we'd take a linebacker, and there are some decent linebackers there. . . . I don't really see us taking a safety this year.

"We'll just have to wait and see who the twenty-one players are that go before we draft."

Straight from the horse's mouth. *Mock Draft: Ed King, OG, Auburn.*

The Miami Dolphins draft number 23. Coach Don Shula has won more NFL games than any coach in history save George Halas, who coached the Bears for forty years, and he is the man in Miami who weighs the scouting reports and then decides. If there is a wide receiver available in the mode of the Dolphins' aging stars, Mark Duper and Mark Clayton, Shula says he will probably take him in the first round. After all, with Dan Marino and his multimillion-dollar arm at quarterback, passing is *the* Dolphins' game.

Would he trade up for the Rocket? No comment. Has he talked at all to New England? "Everybody has." It is never easy to read Don Shula.

A linebacker and a good pass-rushing defensive end are also expressed priorities. But up front . . . *Mock Draft: Randal Hill, WR, Miami (Florida).*

Don Pierson, writing in the *Chicago Tribune:* "If anyone takes a flyer on USC badboy QB Todd Marinovich, why not the Raiders?" Many others feel that the silver and black, notorious badboys themselves, are in dire need of a quarterback and that Marinovich would fit in very nicely.

Owner Al Davis, who by far logged more time scrutinizing the meat at the National Invitational Camp in February than any other owner, makes the decisions here, but he does listen to coach Art Shell.

If Davis does not take a chance with Marinovich in the first round—and almost everyone feels he will be around when the Raiders exercise the twenty-fourth selection in the draft—it is expected that he will go for an offensive lineman, if a decent one is left. Or perhaps a running back; it is known he likes Nick Bell of Iowa, despite the fact that he picked up the San Francisco 49ers' Roger Craig in Plan B. Davis, of course, is one of the most unpredictable people in the NFL.

Maybe he will just trade the pick away. Or maybe he will take a kicker. And the next question is: If he does not take Todd Marinovich, who will? The guess is he will. *Mock Draft: Todd Marinovich, QB, Southern Cal.*

The San Francisco 49ers, without Pro Bowlers safety Ronnie Lott and running back Roger Craig, lost to Plan B, may want to fill those two holes. But the thought among Bear mock drafters is that the 49ers will probably just take the best athlete available, regardless of position, or that they'll trade down.

In the post–Bill Walsh era, the draft decisions are made by the duet of coach George Seifert and general manager John McVay. Seifert is known to have some disturbing questions about his offensive line, so there is speculation San Francisco might trade up to get one of the plums at that position.

San Francisco, it is believed, could go one of many ways with the twenty-fifth choice. *Mock Draft: Trade; if not—Harvey Williams, RB, Louisiana State.*

The Buffalo Bills, it would seem, do not need much, coming out of the 1990 season with the best record in the AFC (13–3–0), breezing through the playoffs, and then losing a squeaker of a Super Bowl to the New York Giants, 20–19.

Defensive back and wide receiver are areas of consideration. So is linebacker.

The Bills draft by committee. Chairman is general manager Bill Pollan; members include coach Marv Levy, player personnel chief John Butler, assistant general manager Bob Ferguson, and, last but not least, owner Ralph Wilson.

The Bear brain trust thinks that the Bills will merely exercise the luxury of drafting the best athlete still around. *Mock Draft: Alfred Williams, LB, Colorado.*

The Super Bowl champion New York Giants have been shrewd drafters during the 1980s, but that hasn't always been the case for the Mara family. During the 1960s and '70s, the Giants were plagued with poor choices who never panned out or lived up to their billing. These days, the draft choices are made by mutual agreement between general manager George Young, and coach Bill Parcells (who is working his last draft because, although no one knows it yet, he will retire shortly after this one.)

The Giants, because of age and injuries, perhaps need more than the team they defeated in the Super Bowl three months earlier. All-Pro tight end Mark Bavaro is a big question mark because of a career-threatening injury in 1990, but there are no tempting first-round tight ends in the 1991 crop. Wide receiver is the most likely position they will consider, partly because that crop is one of the best in the 1991 draft.

The Giants' linebacking corps, showcasing sure-to-be Hall of Famer Lawrence Taylor, one of the greatest for many years, is getting a little on the elderly side. Somewhere later in the draft the Giants will take one.

But like Buffalo, the Giants will undoubtedly just grab the best player they can get with this, the last pick of the first round of the 1991 draft. *Mock Draft: Kelvin Pritchett, DT, Mississippi.*

MOCK DRAFTS

Here are two other mock drafts from top pro football analysts that appeared the week before D-Day. There are only twenty-seven first-round picks, because the New York Jets gave up theirs (what would have been the eighth) so they could take Syracuse wide receiver Rob Moore in the previous summer's supplemental draft.

Joel Buchsbaum, *Pro Football Weekly*

Pick	Team	Player	Position	College
1	New England	Raghib Ismail	WR	Notre Dame
2	Cleveland	Todd Lyght	CB	Notre Dame
3	Atlanta	Mike Croel	LB	Nebraska
4	Denver	Antone Davis	OT	Tennessee
5	L.A. Rams	Russell Maryland	DT	Miami (Florida)
6	Phoenix	Charles McRae	OT	Tennessee
7	Tampa Bay	Eric Turner	S	UCLA
8	Green Bay	Nick Bell	RB	Iowa
9	San Diego	Bruce Pickens	CB	Nebraska
10	Detroit	Ted Washington	DT	Louisville

Joel Buchsbaum, Pro Football Weekly *(cont.)*

Pick	Team	Player	Position	College
11	Dallas	Pat Harlow	OT	Southern Cal
12	Dallas	Alfred Williams	LB	Colorado
13	Kansas City*	Alvin Harper	WR	Tennessee
14	Dallas	Bobby Wilson	DT	Michigan State
15	Pittsburgh	Herman Moore	WR	Virginia
16	Seattle	Randal Hill	WR	Miami (Florida)
17	Houston	Stanley Richard	S	Texas
18	Cincinnati	Huey Richardson	DE	Florida
19	Philadelphia	Stan Thomas	OT	Texas
20	Washington	Aaron Craver	RB	Fresno State
21	Atlanta*	Vince Clark	CB	Ohio State
22	Chicago	Chris Thome	C	Minnesota
23	Miami	Wesley Carroll	WR	Miami (Florida)
24	L.A. Raiders	Todd Marinovich	QB	Southern Cal
25	San Francisco	Leonard Russell	RB	Arizona State
26	Buffalo	Eric Swann	DE	(no college)
27	N.Y. Giants	Keith Traylor	LB	Central State (Oklahoma)

*Predicted switch in draft order due to trade between Atlanta and Kansas City.

Mel Kiper, ESPN

Pick	Team	Player	Position	College
1	Atlanta*	Raghib Ismail	WR	Notre Dame
2	Cleveland	Todd Lyght	CB	Notre Dame
3	New England*	Antone Davis	OT	Tennessee
4	Denver	Mike Croel	LB	Nebraska
5	L.A. Rams	Russell Maryland	DT	Miami (Florida)
6	Phoenix	Charles McRae	OT	Tennessee
7	Tampa Bay	Eric Turner	S	UCLA

Pick	Team	Player	Position	College
8	Green Bay	Nick Bell	RB	Iowa
9	San Diego	Alvin Harper	WR	Tennessee
10	Detroit	Herman Moore	WR	Virginia
11	Dallas	Huey Richardson	DE	Florida
12	Dallas	Pat Harlow	OT	Southern Cal
13	Atlanta	Bruce Pickens	CB	Nebraska
14	Dallas	Eric Swann	DE	(no college)
15	Pittsburgh	Reggie Barrett	WR	Texas–El Paso
16	Seattle	Dan McGwire	QB	San Diego State
17	Houston	Stanley Richard	S	Texas
18	Cincinnati	Ted Washington	DT	Louisville
19	Philadelphia	Harvey Williams	RB	Louisiana State
20	Washington	Leonard Russell	RB	Arizona State
21	Kansas City	Mike Pritchard	WR	Colorado
22	Chicago	Kelvin Pritchett	DT	Mississippi
23	Miami	Randal Hill	WR	Miami (Florida)
24	L.A. Raiders	Todd Marinovich	QB	Southern Cal
25	San Francisco	Vince Clark	CB	Ohio State
26	Buffalo	Mike Dumas	S	Indiana
27	N.Y. Giants	Jeff Graham	WR	Ohio State

*Predicted switch in draft order due to trade between New England and Atlanta.

THE DRAFT

The big news comes two days before D-Day. The New England Patriots are finally able to work a deal they can live with and trade the number one pick to Dallas for one of the Cowboys' first-round (number 11) and second-round (number 28) choices in 1991, with three Cowboy veterans thrown in for good measure—linebackers Eugene Lockhart and David Howard and defensive back Ron Francis.

It appears Rocket Ismail will be streaking down the AstroTurf of Texas Stadium, in the footsteps of such explosive Cowboy wide receivers of yore as Bob Hayes, Drew Pearson, and Tony Hill.

The bigger news comes the night after. Raghib Ismail now has a new nickname—Draft Dodger—because he decides that he would rather streak down the larger football fields of Canada than those of the USA.

Rocket Ismail has signed with the Toronto Argonauts, a franchise of the Canadian Football League owned principally by Bruce McNall (60 percent), hockey superstar Wayne Gretzky (20 percent), and portly actor/comedian John Candy (20 percent).

The story of the Rocket's decision to defect to Canada is a quirky one, with allegations coming from various sides. Dave

Anderson wrote in his column for the *New York Times* that Ismail was insulted during contract negotiations with the New England Patriots when their personnel director, Joe Mendes, said the Rocket had "the attention span of Tim Worley," a running back for the Steelers who is said to be markedly short in that department.

Another rumor was that Mendes made a racist remark during their talks, which Ismail would later say was untrue. The Rocket did say, however, that he thought the NFL teams he talked to "treated me like a piece of meat." McNall, on the other hand, brought him up to Toronto in a style only European royalty or Las Vegas high rollers are accustomed to. Then he brought him to Los Angeles to watch Gretzky play for the Kings, after which the two owners allegedly took Rocket and Toronto quarterback Matt Dunigan on a $10,000 shopping spree on tony Rodeo Drive in Beverly Hills. McNall transported the Rocket from place to place via a private jet and a chauffeur-driven Rolls-Royce. "They treated me like a friend of the family," Ismail said. Later: "Those folks could see the fiber of my being."

They also offered him a *guaranteed* contract worth $18.2 million over four years, which prompted Howard Balzer, a correspondent for *Pro Football Weekly*, to write: "Don't get me wrong, there's nothing wrong with going for the bucks. But, then, don't start feeding us those lines about a special bond with Bruce McNall and that they treated him as more than a piece of meat. Be serious, Raghib. If Dallas or New England had matched McNall's money, you'd be telling us how you either love Remington shavers [the company owned by Patriot owner Victor Kiam] or will join Jimmy Johnson [Cowboy coach] drinking beer with ice cubes [the coach's predilection]."

Perhaps it was best summed up when Ismail's mother, Fatma, was asked how she felt about her son going to play football in a foreign country and she replied, "I said, 'Honey, get on that freedom train and let's go!' "

Ismail will be earning more each year than the entire roster of players and coaches of any single team in the CFL because the financially troubled league has been operating under a $3 million team salary cap. McNall got around the cap by claiming the generous money the Rocket is to receive is under a "personal services contract," and not salary as such. The highest single salary in the CFL the year before, incidentally, was the $335,000 McNall paid to his quarterback, Matt Dunigan.

Ismail, of course, is not the first U.S. player to choose Canada over the NFL. Billy Vessels, Heisman Trophy–winning halfback from Oklahoma, gained that distinction when he signed with the Edmonton Eskimos in 1953. All-America Notre Dame quarterback Joe Theismann opted for the Toronto Argonauts in 1970, and another Heisman winner, wide receiver/kick returner Johnny Rodgers of Nebraska, chose the Montreal Alouettes in 1973. Linebacker Tom Cousineau of Ohio State, who was the number one pick in the 1979 NFL draft, instead signed with the Alouettes. Other players to have chosen Canada include running backs Terry Metcalf and Anthony Davis, and quarterbacks Tobin Rote and Warren Moon. Some of these players, of course, later switched to the NFL.

The Rocket's choice is certainly a topic of conversation at Bear headquarters this D-Day morning. His shunning of the NFL has no real impact here, however, because the Bears were not interested in him in the first place. But those sitting around the conference room in Halas Hall—one of its walls now festooned with tabs bearing names and grades: *the* lists that Bill Tobin has been arranging, rearranging, and guarding for the past several weeks—are curious as to how this will affect the draft, which will start in just a few hours.

So the morning of D-Day is one of speculation. Who will Dallas now take with its newly won first pick?

The answer is revealed when the Cowboys select Russell Maryland of Miami (Florida). Most of those in the war room at Halas

Hall are surprised. Rod Graves, who has scouted Maryland, expected the big but relatively short (6'1") defensive tackle to go among the first five, but not number one. "I thought he was the best defensive lineman in the draft, but we had some other players with higher grades than Russell," he said.

One person who is not surprised is Bill Tobin. "Not with Jimmy Johnson's connection with Russell and Miami," Tobin said, referring to the fact that Johnson had recruited and coached Maryland for two years at Miami before he became head coach of the Cowboys.

The most pleasant surprise, however, is received by Russell Maryland and his agent Leigh Steinberg (who, incidentally, is the agent for the two preceding number one picks in the draft— quarterbacks Troy Aikman of Dallas and Jeff George of Indianapolis), in the form of a five-year contract worth about $1.5 million a year, which is about $600,000 a year more than Maryland would have gotten if he had gone as the number five selection that most of the mock drafters had slotted him for.

Maryland, who carried 325 pounds on his 6'1" frame as a high school senior, received the last scholarship offered by Jimmy Johnson as head coach at Miami in 1988. And it was only awarded, ironically enough, after Chris Zorich had turned down Miami in favor of Notre Dame. Between Zorich choosing Notre Dame and Notre Dame's Rocket Ismail choosing the CFL over the NFL, the school with the Golden Dome and the ghosts of Knute Rockne, George Gipp, and the Four Horsemen has had a decided influence on the career and fortunes of Russell Maryland.

Urged on by potential agents and various team scouts, he had considered going into the NFL supplemental draft, held the previous spring. But he was dissuaded by his father. "Russell wasn't mature enough or emotionally ready to take that great step," his father, Jim Maryland, said. "I told him to wait. But it wasn't like I was blocking my son's goals. He didn't want to desert his college team. Also, he probably wouldn't have been any higher than a second-rounder.'' Good—and profitable—advice, as it turned out.

Maryland, a Chicagoan, watched the draft from his agent's home in Newport Beach, California. Just before he went out there, Maryland was in Chicago and, for nostalgia's sake, traced the path where he used to jog on the city's dangerous South Side in an effort to lose enough weight so that he could get a decent college scholarship. He lost fifty pounds on the path. "I wanted to remember where it all started.''

What it also got him, besides a slimmer body, was the honor of becoming the first Chicago high school football player ever to be the number one selection in the NFL draft.

But being the first pick in the draft is no guarantee of success in the NFL. Admittedly, there have been number ones like O. J. Simpson, Terry Bradshaw, Too Tall Jones, Lee Roy Selmon, and Earl Campbell in the past twenty or so years. But there have also been the likes of Walt Patulski, defensive end from Notre Dame, who had the honor in 1972 and had a disappointing and short career with the Buffalo Bills.

Then there was Ricky Bell in 1977, All-America running back out of Southern Cal who had one good year in the NFL (1979, when he gained 1,263 yards), but otherwise was a bust. And Ken Sims, the highly touted defensive end from Texas who topped the list in 1982; he spent almost as much time on injured reserve as he did on the playing field for the New England Patriots. Irving Fryar, wide receiver from Nebraska, was the premier draft pick of 1984 and so far has proven to be a bigger pain in the neck to the Patriots than anyone, even a number one, should be. Then there was Auburn's dazzling running back Bo Jackson, who chose major league baseball over carrying the football for the Tampa Bay Buccaneers, who drafted him first in 1986. And linebacker Aundray Bruce, another product of Auburn, who headed the 1988 NFL draft, never did anything noteworthy for the Atlanta Falcons. He was later converted to tight end and has since moved on to the Los Angeles Raiders.

There is a lot that should, but often does not, come after the hype of D-Day when you are chosen number one.

The choice of Russell Maryland as number one is only the first surprise of several in the first six picks of the 1991 draft. In fact, the first six selections collectively will be a surprise, because they will all be defensive players. Before 1991, the most defensive players ever taken consecutively at the beginning of a draft was a mere three, first in 1982 when the Patriots took defensive end Ken Sims, the Colts took linebacker Johnie Cooks, and the Browns selected linebacker Chip Banks; and then in 1988 when linebacker Aundray Bruce went first to Atlanta, defensive end Neil Smith second to Kansas City, and safety Bennie Blades third to Detroit.

It is not a surprise when the Browns, drafting second, take a defensive back; just about everybody had predicted they would. The surprise comes when NFL commissioner Paul Tagliabue announces it is UCLA safety Eric Turner—not Notre Dame cornerback Todd Lyght, the National Scouting Combine's second highest graded player in the entire draft. General manager Ernie Accorsi says the Browns graded the hard-hitting Turner very high and believe he will be the NFL's next Ronnie Lott. Trivium: According to Neil Warner, managing editor of *Pro Football Weekly*, there has not been a defensive back chosen as early as number two in the NFL draft since Gary Glick was the first selection of the 1956 draft, taken by the Pittsburgh Steelers.

Surprise number three: The Atlanta Falcons skip over both Todd Lyght and premier linebacker Mike Croel and take Nebraska cornerback Bruce Pickens. Pickens had gotten high numbers from the Bears, but they did not think he would go so soon—of course, neither had they thought Eric Turner would be number two. But in the first round of the draft, as Jim Parmer notes, "There are always one helluva lot of surprises"—not usually, however, in the first three picks.

The Denver Broncos hardly hesitate after the Falcons take Pickens. They were planning, it was thought, on taking an offensive lineman, but that was because they did not believe Croel would be there. Inside their war room out in Denver, a few words are passed, then coach Dan Reeves sends the call out quickly to their man in New York—take Mike Croel.

The touted Todd Lyght of Notre Dame is finally remembered on the fifth pick, when he is selected by the Los Angeles Rams. It is a surprise in one way, but not in another. Yes, the Rams have been hoping for a defensive lineman (Russell Maryland, that is) and are in need of a good offensive lineman, and none of that certified-quality crop has yet been touched; but in Lyght they take the player who coach John Robinson feels is the best athlete available, and who to his way of thinking, has been unwisely ignored by those who have drafted ahead of the Rams.

The cadre in the Bear war room is not surprised by the Rams' decision—they had Todd Lyght highly graded and Bill Tobin knows that the relatively conservative drafter John Robinson has often put position priorities behind the philosophy of taking the best athlete available.

Michael McCaskey and Bill Tobin express some mild astonishment that three defensive backs have been taken among the first five selections, certainly the first time that has ever happened in the fifty-five-year history of the draft. But the Bears are also pleased with the direction of the draft because, so far, their priorities have been untapped—except, of course, for Russell Maryland, but they never figured he would be there when their pick came up anyway.

The deals that will characterize this draft day have not yet been made, or at least not yet announced. But telephones are ringing in war rooms throughout the National Football League, especially in light of the fact that the first five draft choices have all been defensive players, and somewhat surprising ones at that. There is a lot of talk about trading up or down, a lot of scrambling now. Bill Tobin fields the calls for the Bears. He talks with the San Diego Chargers, who draft ninth—they called, not he. He talks with the Dallas Cowboys, who, at this point, still have two first-round choices well ahead of the Bears to barter with—they called, but they are calling *everybody*. Tobin is content to wait and see what goes down as the draft continues to unfold in its so-far unorthodox fashion. Tobin makes a few calls himself, but more to find out what is going on, maybe get a feel as to how the order of the draft may change and therefore affect the Bears' situation down the line, than to curry deals.

The biggest shock comes with the sixth selection. The Phoenix Cardinals take defensive end Eric Swann, the only player in the draft without college football experience. Most mock drafts had him going in the second or third round, some even later. "A risky choice," McCaskey observes, "but, who knows, maybe a few years from now it will be considered a gamble that paid off, an excellent selection."

Rod Graves had studied Swann as best he could without college game films to aid him, and had graded him. "I did not feel he had shown enough talent to be considered a first-round draft choice. He has good physical [6'4" and a weight that has varied between 280 and 310 pounds over the past two years] and athletic tools [a 4:90 in the 40]. But there is a great margin of risk with anyone who has not played major college competition. I had him as draftable maybe in the third round."

Jim Parmer notes, "I was surprised *who* drafted him. The Cardinals are not a real gambling team in a thing like this. But then, they haven't drafted well in a long time. They're notorious for ending up with somebody from out in left field. I think maybe they reached out into left field again. I'm pretty sure we wouldn't have drafted the kid if he was there when the twenty-second pick came up."

The proximity of Las Vegas to the Cardinals' new home may have had something to do with it, maybe sending a germ of gambling fever across the desert that infiltrated the Phoenix camp. Who knows? At any rate, mammoth Eric Swann is logged in as the sixth consecutive defensive player in the first six rounds of the 1991 draft.

The string is broken, however, by the Tampa Bay Buccaneers when they select offensive tackle Charles McRae. Most people, the Bears included, had thought his teammate on the front line at Tennessee, Antone Davis, would have gone before McRae.

Tampa Bay's choice triggers the first trade of the day. The Green Bay Packers, who draft next, are on the phone, listening to an offer from the Philadelphia Eagles they apparently cannot refuse. The Eagles, scheduled to draft nineteenth in the first round, want to move up and snatch Antone Davis, who they had graded the best offensive lineman available but had not expected to linger until the eighth pick.

It is costly, however. The Shylock Packers want Philadelphia's first-round choice this year and its first-round choice in 1992. The Eagles, adopting the controversial strategy of "Pick now, pay later," agree to the deal, and Antone Davis is destined to launch his pro football career in the City of Brotherly Love.

More than a few eyebrows are raised when the purchase price is announced. But Philadelphia director of player personnel Joe Wooley defends it: "Anytime you can have a guy for a year and not have to pay for it, you help yourself. Worry about this year, don't worry about next year. You only play one year at a time."

Bobby Beathard, the wheeling-dealing general manager out in San Diego, takes very little of the fifteen minutes allotted to him to make the ninth selection. His man in New York hands Tagliabue the slip of paper in under five minutes, and, as was predicted in a lot of circles, Texas safety Stanley Richard becomes a Charger.

Beathard remarked later, "He was one of the two highest-rated players on our charts. The other was Antone Davis, and with him already gone, the decision was already made for us. We were just delighted that Stanley was still around. I could easily have seen him going earlier, too.''

The Bears also had Stanley Richard graded very high, but safety is not one of their chief priorities this year. Still, it would have been awfully difficult not to take him if he had lasted.

The tenth pick is no surprise at all either. The Detroit Lions are admittedly in the market for a wide receiver, and all the best are there for the choosing. They decide to take the imposing (6'4", 205-pound) Herman Moore from Virginia.

While all this has been going on, the Dallas Cowboys' phones have been as busy as those of one of Damon Runyon's Broadway bookmakers. Owner Jerry Jones and coach Jimmy Johnson are hardly content with merely trading up to get the first pick in the draft from New England. They seem motivated to try to make the late trade baron George Allen of the Rams and Redskins appear as conservative as Calvin Coolidge.

It gets a little complicated, but here is what they have been up to this D-Day. First, they negotiate another trade with the New England Patriots: New England gets the Cowboys' fourteenth pick in the first round and Dallas gets the seventeenth pick from the Patriots, which New England had acquired the previous Friday from the Houston Oilers, New England giving Houston in return the first pick in the second round (twenty-eighth overall) and the eighteenth in the fourth round (101st overall) of this year's draft.

Still with us?

Then Dallas trades its just-acquired seventeenth pick in the first round to the Washington Redskins for the twentieth pick in the first round and a fifth-round choice. And lastly, which is a bit down the line, it will choose a player with that twentieth pick and then trade the rights to him to the Detroit Lions for a pick in each of the second, third, and fourth rounds.

And this is just in the first round. No wonder the Cowboys have always banked on computers.

New England is up next, exercising the eleventh selection, which it acquired from—who else—the Dallas Cowboys in the previous Friday's transaction, the one that allegedly was going to put Rocket Ismail in a Cowboy uniform.

In one of NFL life's little ironies, the Patriots draft the very same player the Cowboys were planning to draft with the next pick, the only one of their original three that they have retained. He is the highly regarded offensive tackle from Southern Cal, Pat Harlow.

As far as the Bears are concerned—and they are getting mildly concerned—the stock of top-drawer offensive linemen is dwindling fast, with three of them now accounted for and ten more choices coming up before Chicago's turn to draft. But then Bill Tobin never drafts by priority alone, and there remain a number of very good ballplayers still untaken who carry high Bear grades. Wish-list names are being spoken for to Michael McCaskey and Mike Ditka by the scouts and Tobin. They are constantly going over them—among them offensive tackle Stan Thomas of Texas, defensive end Huey Richardson of Florida, defensive tackle Kelvin Pritchett of Mississippi, wide receiver Mike Pritchard of Colorado, and various others.

In Dallas, despite all the Cowboys' other convoluted dealings, they do remember to respond and make the twelfth pick of the draft. With Pat Harlow having been snatched by the ungrateful Patriots, they go to another priority, wide receiver, and choose Alvin Harper of Tennessee. Then the two JJs rush back to the phones, or at least we so conjecture; after all, there are fifteen more picks in the first round, not to mention the eleven other rounds to come in the 1991 draft—a lot can be bought or shed in the barter bazaar before it finally closes down when the New York Giants take the 334th and final pick of the 1991 draft.

Picking thirteenth is Atlanta. With the Falcons' second selection of the day, they choose a player the Bears had highly graded and one they thought, or at least hoped, might not go so early—

150

wide receiver Mike Pritchard of Colorado. A lot of people thought he might end up going to the Bears if the well-graded offensive and defensive linemen had been depleted by the twenty-second pick.

New England, with its second selection of round one, the result of its trade with Dallas earlier in the day, decides to take the first back in the draft, Leonard Russell of Arizona State. He has both size and speed and the reputation for being considerably difficult to bring down, and therefore seems to be a natural to make it in the hard-hitting NFL.

At stop number 15 on the D-Day line, the Pittsburgh Steelers rake off another player for whom the Bears definitely had eyes. It is defensive end or possible linebacker Huey Richardson of Florida, who Rod Graves had graded especially high and hoped might be overlooked in the first twenty-one selections.

It comes as no great surprise when the Seattle Seahawks take the first quarterback in this year's draft, the rangy Dan McGwire of San Diego State. Seattle may have just drafted what may be the tallest quarterback in the history of the NFL; McGwire is 6'8", and should have no problem seeing over his blockers and opposing pass rushers. Seattle also had a shot at quarterbacks Brett Favre of Southern Mississippi and Browning Nagle of Louisville, both of whom the Seahawks were considering, but decided McGwire's size and his acknowledged strong-arm passing (he threw for 3,833 yards and twenty-seven touchdowns his senior year) rated the nod.

The Washington Redskins, up next thanks to a trade with—who else—the Dallas Cowboys earlier that afternoon, clip another player the Bears would have liked to see hang in until the twenty-second pick. He is defensive tackle Bobby Wilson from Michigan State.

The Cincinnati Bengals then take linebacker Alfred Williams of Colorado, a good choice for them, or so many believe. And a welcome choice for the Bear enclave, because it was thought that Cincinnati might grab an offensive lineman.

At this point, the Bears know who they are going to draft if he is still there. Granted, there may be some last-minute discussion. But if Green Bay, Dallas, or Kansas City do not take him, offensive tackle Stan Thomas from Texas, a 300-pounder who did not allow a single sack his senior year and is considered a fearsome run blocker, is the man. No one's fingers are more tightly crossed at this point than those of Jim Parmer, who scouted Thomas and has read on him to McCaskey and Ditka earlier in the day and is getting ready to do so again.

At this point, the Bears feel sort of good about their chances, because they do not believe that the Packers or the Chiefs are especially looking for an offensive lineman. The Cowboys may be, but it was Pat Harlow they wanted, and they lost him by a single pick to the Patriots. It is not known if they want Thomas— but then he is, after all, from their state. And so there is some question here.

Still, the call goes out from Bear headquarters down to Thomas's home in Texas. The Bears have his telephone number and know that he will be at that number on draft day, thanks to the assiduous research Rod Graves has done over the preceding weeks in pinning down that kind of information so the Bears can talk to a prospect before they go on the line and draft him.

That's the way it is done in the 1990s. "We want to make sure he didn't get hit by a truck the night before," Bill Tobin says wryly, but it is something more than that. When Thomas gets on the phone, he hears a voice he will hear a lot more of if things work out for the Bears a few picks down the line. "This is Mike Ditka; we are thinking of taking you with our first-round pick." The questions are brief. Do you have any problem with playing in Chicago? Under the Bears' system? Things like that.

Stan Thomas answers them. He says he would be thrilled to play in Chicago, thrilled to play for the Bears.

Then it is back to waiting. The Green Bay Packers are still thinking about who to take. They have the nineteenth pick as a result of their trade with the Eagles a number of rounds earlier. The Packers have always been a major pain to the Bears, archrivals since 1921, when the Pack first traveled down to Wrigley Field in Chicago to get trounced 20–0. (Green Bay, however, has returned the favor a number of times over the ensuing seven decades. At the time of this draft, the Bears had won eighty of their encounters with the Packers, lost fifty-seven, and tied six.)

This time, however, the Packers oblige the Bears. They take cornerback Vince Clark of Ohio State, the fifth defensive back taken thus far. The Packers are as happy with this selection as the Bears are, because the secondary is where Green Bay has had real problems in the last couple of years. And the Packers still have Philadelphia's selection in the first round of next year's draft.

The countdown with the Cowboys seems a lot longer than fifteen minutes, but it is not. The Jones/Johnson Trading Company of Dallas does it again. It drafts defensive tackle Kelvin Pritchett of Mississippi and immediately turns around and trades the rights to him to the Detroit Lions for a choice in each of the next three rounds. A sigh of relief echoes out from the war room at Halas Hall.

The Kansas City Chiefs surprise everyone. It was figured by most that they would take a quarterback or a wide receiver. Instead they select running back Harvey Williams of Louisiana State. And this is a team that already has three running backs who in one season or another have rushed for more than a thousand yards (Christian Okoye, Stump Mitchell, and Barry Word). The speedy Williams, however, is also a very good kick and punt returner, an added asset.

The Bears do not have time to think of Kansas City's surprise. They are busy finalizing their pick. There had been some lobbying for taking Notre Dame defensive tackle Chris Zorich in the first round. Ditka does not want him to get away. But the consensus of opinion is that they can wait on him and still get him somewhere down the line.

The choice: Stan Thomas.

Thomas is thrilled, Jim Parmer elated, the Bear staff quite happy with the way things have worked out.

"I think I'll be a starter—maybe not the first game, but I think I will before the season's over," Thomas said when he learned he was in fact the Bears' first-round choice. "The Bears intimidate people on the field, and that is the kind of football I like. I think I'm the kind of Bear offensive lineman who gets after it, a guy who is very aggressive on the run. I'm kind of known for going out on the field and getting after people. Some people don't like that. But that is what football is all about."

In regard to his new coach, Thomas said, "I look forward to playing for coach Ditka. I like those kind of coaches that get after you. If you make a mistake, he is going to let you know." That was perhaps *the* understatement of D-Day.

It is not as if it is just some kind of D-Day decision, however. The Bears had been interested in Thomas for quite some time. As Bill Tobin explains, "Parmer scouted him for three years, read on him several times. Rod Graves cross-checked him. I went down to Texas and saw him. So we had three Bear reports on him, six BLESTO reports, a bowl game report. We really worked on Thomas, especially during the spring of his junior year and throughout his senior year. We were more than a little familiar with him. We had no trouble with a consensus on him."

"I was real happy about the choice," Jim Parmer said after it was over. "I really liked Stan. The year before, though, I thought he had a lot of dog in him. He really didn't play up to his capability. I thought from what I saw he'd take a play off from time to time. Even good ones do that, but great ones hardly ever.

"Stan's a pretty smart kid, though. I went in there down in Austin in the spring [of his junior year]. He knew I was in there looking pretty closely at him. So he says he wants to meet me, says that way I can get a damn good look at him.

"We sat down for about an hour. Right off he says, very nicely though, 'Would you mind telling me what you think about me?' And I told him. 'Stan, the biggest thing I see wrong with you—and I'm gonna be honest with you as long as *you* asked *me*—your motor don't run all the time.' And he said he'd heard something like that before, and just to watch him next year.

"Course then he came around. I went over there the next fall and I could see he was having just a helluva year. I saw nothing that I saw the year before. He wasn't taking plays off, was playing well, consistently well. I thought he had a little nasty in him. I don't think he is a mean kid, but he is a halfway mean football player. And by the season's end I knew I could read on him with a lot of heart.

"And believe me, you do have to read for a kid, especially with the Bears. You just can't say, 'Here's my grade, I'd draft him.' You have to be a good salesman, you have to sell Mc-Caskey and Ditka—and they aren't easy sells; McCaskey's always got a ton of questions. But if you do it right, maybe you get the kid drafted."

When Parmer did read to McCaskey, Ditka, Tobin, and the other scouts, he mentioned that Thomas started at right tackle every game for three years at Texas and even one game as a freshman, and that his senior year he was named to the All-Southwest Conference team.

Well, apparently Jim Parmer did it right, and all the other reports, most importantly Bill Tobin's, fell in line. What Tobin had to say was this, "Pass protection is one of his best assets right now. He's a smart kid who's going to graduate on time. He's played in a major program and he has good practice habits."

"There's a lot of work that goes into this," Michael McCaskey adds, "from Bill Tobin, the scouts, the coaching staff, and we think we are one of the very best at it, if not the best." It's hard to argue with when you see Bear teams over the past decade who, except for a year or two, have been serious playoff contenders, once a Super Bowl champion, and were built almost exclusively from the draft.

And so with Stan Thomas in the Bears' den, the first round winds down. The Miami Dolphins also get who they want, wide receiver Randal Hill, who played college ball in Miami. The Los Angeles Raiders do take the chance and draft quarterback Todd Marinovich of Southern Cal.

The San Francisco 49ers take the sometimes sluggish defensive tackle Ted Washington out of Louisville. Buffalo opts for Henry Jones of Illinois, who they think can play either cornerback or safety in the NFL. And finally, the world champion New York Giants choose massive, hard-blocking fullback Jarrod Bunch of Michigan.

And so the first round ends. Who were the most popular this year? Defensive backs, with six being selected in the first round; next defensive linemen, with five going; followed by wide receivers and offensive linemen, four each; then running backs and linebackers, three each; and finally quarterbacks, two of them.

Some of the meat went a lot higher than the analysts and mock drafters had predicted, and some high-graders were surprisingly ignored. Where, in fact, was wide receiver Reggie Barrett, who the National Scouting Combine graded 8.2, highest of any player eligible for the 1991 draft?

And there were eight trades that affected the order of the first round of what will be remembered as one of the NFL's most swap-filled drafts ever.

Well, there are still three more rounds left today, D-Day, and eight more tomorrow.

The second round does not possess the glamour of the first, nor does it get the press and media coverage, but it is still all pretty much prime meat there.

The Houston Oilers, who obtained the first pick in the second round (twenty-eighth overall) in a trade with the New England

Patriots, are delighted to find cornerback-turned-free-safety Mike Dumas of Indiana still there, because a defensive back is precisely what headed their wish-list. Dumas graded highest at safety in the National Scouting Combine ratings, ahead of both Eric Turner, the draft's second selectee, and Stanley Richard, who was the ninth pick of the first round.

The Cleveland Browns next take junior-eligible offensive guard Ed King of Auburn, who the Bears had more than a slight interest in but did not figure to be a first-rounder. (Rod Graves thought if King had played out his senior year, however, he might have gone in the first half of the first round in 1992.)

The first tight end of the draft to be selected is Reggie Johnson of Florida State, claimed by the Denver Broncos. Dan Reeves says he likes the 256-pounder because of his superb blocking ability.

The Rams, with the fourth pick of this round, take UCLA linebacker Roman Phifer, highly regarded as a pass rusher. Coach John Robinson says he thinks Phifer may see action right away in sure passing situations.

The Phoenix Cardinals seem addicted to defensive ends in this draft. After taking Eric Swann in the first round, they select a smaller Mike Jones of North Carolina State here in the second.

Brett Favre of Southern Mississippi, who a lot of the experts thought would go in the first round, is claimed by the Atlanta Falcons. According to Joel Buchsbaum of *Pro Football Weekly*, this "was one of the biggest steals of the draft."

The New York Jets, exercising their first pick in this year's draft, follow suit and claim a quarterback, Browning Nagle from Louisville. The scouting reports praise his arm but also note his lack of mobility.

The Green Bay Packers take defensive lineman Esera Tuaolo of Oregon State. He played nose tackle in college and the Pack plans to convert him to defensive tackle in its 4–3 defense.

Another defensive tackle goes as the ninth pick of the second round when the San Diego Chargers take George Thornton of Alabama. He is the sixth defensive tackle to be selected. The Bears are hoping no more are grabbed because the next logical one would be Chris Zorich, and we all know how Mike Ditka feels about the kid who would pay to play for the Bears.

With a pick that Dallas got from Detroit, the Cowboys add a linebacker, Dixon Edwards of Michigan State. Coach Jimmy Johnson thinks Edwards, a bit on the small side, may end up as a strong safety.

As the result of a trade, the Houston Oilers get the eleventh pick of this round (from Minnesota via—of course—Dallas). They choose their second defensive back of this round, corner Darryl Lewis of Arizona.

Eric Bieniemy of Colorado becomes the fourth running back to be drafted in 1991, going to San Diego, who got this pick from a trade with Tampa Bay. Bobby Beathard admitted afterwards that he was not really looking for a running back here "but I didn't expect [Bieniemy] to be around and he was just too good to pass on."

Indianapolis, making its first selection in the draft (this is the fourth straight year the Colts have not had a first-round choice), decides on defensive end Shane Curry of Miami (Florida). A lot of people did not think Curry would go this early.

New England has the next pick, thanks to the trade it made with the Cowboys before the draft. The Patriots choose cornerback Jerome Henderson of Clemson, hoping he will bring some strength to one of their weakest areas.

The New Orleans Saints, exercising their only pick in the first four rounds of the 1991 draft, take wide receiver Wesley Carroll of Miami (Florida). Although Miami's other wide receiver, Randal Hill, went in the first round, Carroll led the Hurricanes in pass receptions in 1990, snaring sixty-one.

With a trade just before pick time, the Los Angeles Raiders get Seattle's selection here, because they wanted Iowa running back

Nick Bell. Concerns about a college knee injury kept Bell out of the first round, even though National graded him as the second-best running back in the draft.

Houston, with its third selection in the second round, takes the first center thus far to be drafted, John Flannery of Syracuse. Weighing in at over 300 pounds, Flannery could be an imposing figure in the Oilers' front line.

Running back Ricky Watters becomes the third of Notre Dame's Fighting Irish to join the NFL as a result of the San Francisco 49ers trading up with the Cincinnati Bengals in order to get him. There is certainly a place for him now that Roger Craig has signed with the Raiders (Plan B).

The Pittsburgh Steelers need wide receivers in the worst way, but they could not pass over defensive end Huey Richardson in the first round. So in the second they go for Jeff Graham of Ohio State, who not only catches passes but is also a good punt returner.

There remain only two picks before the Bears take the forty-ninth, and the Bears have been on the telephone to several players. They really do not need to talk to Chris Zorich—they already have the answers from him about his desire to play football in Chicago, his hometown. He is well-known around the city, not only because of his outstanding football career at Notre Dame, but also because of the tragedy he endured a few months earlier when he returned home from the Orange Bowl, where Notre Dame had played Colorado, to discover his mother dead of a heart attack in their home.

The San Diego Chargers get into the trading arena just before the forty-seventh pick, obtaining the selection from the Redskins so they can draft 300-plus-pound offensive guard Eric Moten of Michigan State. They wanted Moten so much, the Chargers gave up their 1992 first-round pick so they could draft him. Expensive. But Moten was National's top-rated guard, and is the first at his position to be selected in the 1991 draft.

When the Philadelphia Eagles announce that they are taking junior-eligible safety Jesse Campbell of North Carolina State, the Bears know they can have Chris Zorich if they want him.

The question is, Do they? Or do they want to wait, because there is the feeling from some in war room that he will still be there in the third round. "I wasn't surprised he was still around in the second round," Jim Parmer said later. "I thought we probably could have gotten him in the third round. . . . I had him about a third-round grade."

Coach Mike Ditka does *not* want to wait, however. In fact, if he were the only one making the decisions in the war room, Zorich would probably already be a Bear and Stan Thomas would next year be wearing colors other than blue and orange.

There is some discussion at the last minute on the topic of Zorich, as there has been all day. "We liked him [Zorich]," Rod Graves said later. "We all felt he was Mike Ditka's type of player. We just didn't know where he would fall, but we did know Mike wanted him in the Bear camp. We played with the idea of waiting until the third round, but Mike sure did not want to take that chance."

As it turned out, neither did Michael McCaskey and Bill Tobin, and so word went out to New York and Chris Zorich's dream came true.

Besides Ditka's talking for Zorich, scout Jeff Shiver had read on him, noting some pretty impressive credentials. As a senior at Notre Dame, the All-America defensive tackle had won the Lombardi Award for the nation's best interior lineman. As a junior, he was named College Lineman of the Year by the Washington, D.C., Touchdown Club, was a finalist for the Lombardi Award, was a consensus All-America (AP, UPI, the *Sporting News*. . .), and was credited with ninety-two tackles, the third most in the nation that year. He started as a sophomore as well. His attitude about the game was right out of the Mike Ditka football guidebook.

Other teams, and the scouting combines, had given him less than high marks, however, because of his size (6'1", 267 pounds) and some concern about the knee he injured in college.

Ditka addressed that after the draft. "He's a producer. This guy is exactly the same height as the other guy who was picked number one in the draft [Russell Maryland], and [Zorich] is in much better physical shape. They got their guy, we got our guy. He's a Bear."

Zorich got the word while at a friend's house in Elkhart, Indiana. "I owe it to my mother. She concocted the deal with George Halas up in heaven. She's the one who hooked up with Papa Bear and cooked this up." Then he added, "I'm excited, I'm elated, I'm walking on water."

Zorich refused requests from the media to be with him during the draft. "I get real intense about these things," he said. "I didn't want to throw anyone through the window."

The second round plays out with the Kansas City Chiefs selecting offensive tackle Joe Valerio of Pennsylvania; the Seattle Seahawks, with a pick they got in a trade with the Raiders, taking wide receiver Doug Thomas of Clemson; the Cincinnati Bengals, gaining this pick from a trade with the 49ers, snaring defensive end Lamar Rogers of Auburn, who the National had rated number one at this position, ahead of first-rounders Huey Richardson and Kelvin Pritchett (others had Richardson pegged as a linebacker and Pritchett as a defensive tackle); the 49ers taking John Johnson, a linebacker out of Clemson; the Buffalo Bills adding defensive end Phil Hansen from North Dakota State; and lastly, the New York Giants choosing linebacker Kanavis McGhee of Colorado.

There were nine trades that affected the order of the second round, bringing the total of D-Day draft trades to seventeen for the first two rounds.

With the close of the second round, most of the prime has been claimed. But where is that wide receiver from Texas–El Paso, the kid named Reggie Barrett, the one National said was the top available athlete in the draft?

Now we enter the Twilight Zone of the questionables and the sleepers. The next two rounds will still have some highly graded players; after that . . . well, here is where the individual team scouts show their value, because from the fifth round on they will have much more influence over the picks through their personal evaluations and salesmanship abilities.

There are some notable drafts in round three, and some surprises. First off, somebody finally finds Reggie Barrett. The Detroit Lions, thanks to a trade with the Los Angeles Rams, take the sizable and speedy wide receiver with the third pick of the third round.

Another player many thought would have been long gone by now is running back Aaron Craver of Fresno State. He is grabbed by the Miami Dolphins, who got this pick, the fifth of the third round, in a trade with the Atlanta Falcons.

Keith Traylor, who the National ranked as the top inside linebacker in this year's draft but who drew skepticism because he was from a small college (Central State), is picked up by Denver with the sixth pick.

But perhaps the biggest surprise comes when the Bears draft junior-eligible placekicker/punter Chris Gardocki of Clemson—a surprise especially to Chicago's placekicker, Kevin Butler, and punter, Maury Buford. Butler, who has been putting his foot to the ball for the Bears since 1985, is the Bears' all-time leading kicker with the most field goals (134) and the best field goal percentage (73.6); in addition, going into the 1991 season, he stands as the Bears' second leading scorer, with 633 points to his credit, behind only Walter Payton, who managed to score 125 touchdowns during his Bear career for a total of 750 points. But Butler did have a problem—in 1990 his kickoffs stunk, leaving the Bears in often awful field position and Mike Ditka in less than a happy mood.

Equally disturbed has to be Maury Buford, who, at this point in his career, is sixth best among active NFL punters with a career 41.4-yard average.

Others astonished certainly included the Chicago media and fans, who had not expected a kicker—albeit a punter, too—in the third round.

"We did not talk about it outside," Michael McCaskey said, "but inside we had been talking about him the entire week before the draft and decided we were definitely interested in him—and we considered some other kickers as well. Gardocki stood out because he was both a placekicker and a punter."

Bill Tobin added, "We thought he was definitely the best in this year's draft, an especially strong leg which would be a big help on kickoffs. We did not take him to use him in both kicking and punting, but somewhere down the road maybe we will utilize him in both."

But maybe it should not have come as that much of a surprise. As Tobin explains, "It's not something new. Back in my Green Bay days I took [kicker] Chester Marcol in the *second* round, and we took Butler in the fourth round in 1985. I'm not at all averse to jumping on a good kicker in the early rounds."

No job is secure, Kevin Butler and Maury Buford; just ask Richard Nixon.

The fourth and final round of phase one of D-Day contains fewer surprises. It leads off with the New England Patriots taking quarterback Scott Zolak of Maryland, who, according to most reports, should have been gone by this time.

The real stunner comes with the one hundredth pick of the draft. Al Davis, always known as being one of the shrewdest maneuverers in NFL circles, take Raghib "Rocket" Ismail for his Los Angeles Raider team, thereby tying the Rocket to the Raiders should things not work out in Canada. For that matter, how long is four years, the length of Rocket's contract? Remember: In 1963

Gil Brandt drafted Navy Heisman Trophy–winning quarterback Roger Staubach, a tenth-round choice who was facing a four-year commitment to the U.S. Navy, but who came back after it to do a little something for the Dallas Cowboy offense.

The Bears, not surprisingly, draft a defensive back in the fourth round—Joe Johnson, a corner, out of North Carolina State, the 105th pick in the 1991 draft. He was a first-team All-Atlantic Coast Conference selection his senior year, and was a four-year starter for the Wolfpack. Rod Graves had scouted him, read on him. Bill Tobin said, "We needed a cornerback. We felt if we didn't get one here, then we were not going to get one at all because the [cornerback] grades dropped off tremendously after the fourth round. Johnson was the best available and maybe we took him a little early, but we couldn't afford to wait around. Also, we thought he might work as a kick-return specialist."

In the fifth round, center Chris Thome of Minnesota, who some speculated the Bears might take as early as the first round, goes to the Minnesota Vikings as the 119th pick of 1991. From all appearances, the Bears did not have the interest in him ascribed to them by others.

They do have interest in a wide receiver, however, and therefore are happy to see Anthony Morgan of Tennessee still available when the 134th selection comes up. "We feel fortunate with Morgan; he's a big-play kind of guy, which is what we need," Bill Tobin said. "We had no intention of taking a wide receiver in the first couple of rounds, even though a lot of people were saying we might, or would. We felt there was a lot of depth in wide receivers in this draft. And we were delighted he fell to us in the fifth round. In fact, he had our highest rating of any wide receiver."

In the sixth round, the Bears run into a little embarrassment. They take running back Darren Lewis of Texas A & M. The problem is not his athletic prowess; the problem is he tested positive for cocaine down at the National Invitational Camp in

Indianapolis in February and the Bears, for some strange reason, had not been aware of that.

"We had some misinformation on this," Bill Tobin said after the finding came out. "We had no idea about it. When we found out, we decided we'd give him a second chance. If he stays straight, he may turn out to be a very good ballplayer. Actually we were not even intending to take a running back here, but we had a high grade on him. We felt he was the best athlete around, significantly higher than anyone else we had on the board at any position at the time we drafted him."

In the seventh round, the Bears go for the quarterback they want to bring into camp with them so they will have four to play off each other. He is Paul Justin of Arizona State, a starter since his sophomore year there, and regarded by many to have the strongest arm coming out of college football. Justin was National's second highest rated quarterback.

"Because we are thin at cornerback," Michael McCaskey says, "we thought we would take another in the eighth round." He is Larry Horton from Texas A & M, where he was a two-year starter at free safety and a well-regarded kickoff and punt returner.

In the ninth round, the Bears go back to their all-time favorite school for drafting from, Notre Dame, taking linebacker Michael Stonebreaker. He led the Fighting Irish in tackles his senior year with ninety-five and made several All-America teams.

In the tenth round, the Bears add another defensive tackle, Tom Backes of Oklahoma, but the plan, according to Mike Ditka, is to convert him to an offensive tackle.

Stacy Long, an offensive guard from Clemson, is their eleventh-round choice, and John Cook, a defensive tackle from Washington, rounds out the 1991 draft for the Chicago Bears.

The work for Bill Tobin and the scouts is not over, however. They now have the chore of going over what is still left out there, and determing who they might like to invite as rookie free agents.

After twelve exhausting rounds of draft, it would seem that every worthwhile player has been taken. But the Bears know that is not true. They have former free agent Jay Hilgenberg at center, and he is a perennial Pro Bowler. And they once found safety Gary Fencik among the unemployed, and he also went to the Pro Bowl. And, well, there have been a lot of fine ones who came out of the free-agency pool.

This year, over the next day or two, the Bear scouting staff and Bill Tobin will pick twenty-three free agents, sign them, and give them the chance to make the team and have a career in the National Football League.

A scant three days after the last pick of the last round of the 1991 draft is taken, the Bears will hold their mini-camp at Halas Hall. And from that moment on, the futures of the 1991 draftees and rookie free agents will fall into their own hands. Some will make it and keep playing the game they love. Others will not and be forced to go out and face life after football.

And Bill Tobin and his scouts will go back out on the road; there is the 1992 draft, after all, and another thousand seniors and juniors who need to be studied and graded . . .

11

HOW
IT ALL
TURNED OUT

The Bears drafted across the board in 1991, filling their greatest needs in the first two rounds, an offensive lineman and a defensive lineman, and in the process getting two players who were very high on their wish-list. The triumvirate—McCaskey/Tobin/Ditka—were extremely pleased with their top two picks. And they were especially happy with the fact that they had no trouble signing either. In fact, first-round pick Stan Thomas was signed within a week after D-Day to a five-year contract reportedly worth $3.25 million, including a $1.2 million signing bonus, making him the second highest paid offensive lineman in Bear history (many-time All-Pro tackle Jim Covert being the first).

Of their twelve draftees, the Bears took three defensive linemen (Chris Zorich, Tom Backes, John Cook), two offensive linemen (Stan Thomas, Stacy Long), and two defensive backs (Joe Johnson, Larry Horton). And they added one each of the following: kicker/punter (Chris Gardocki), wide receiver (Anthony Morgan), running back (Darren Lewis), quarterback (Paul Justin), and linebacker (Michael Stonebreaker).

The rookie free agents were spread around as well.

WIDE RECEIVERS

Sean Becton of Central Florida
Steve Brown of Wake Forest
Nigel Codrington of Rice
Anthony Cummings of Louisville
Michael Johnson of California State/Sacramento
Eric Wright of Stephen F. Austin (Texas)

DEFENSIVE BACKS

Ron Ferguson of Texas Tech (CB)
John Hardy of California (CB)
Tim Lance of Eastern Illinois (S)
Quintin Parker of Illinois (S)
John Wiley of Auburn (S)

LINEBACKERS

Richard Booker of Texas Christian
Peter Brantley of Oregon
Charles Rowe of Texas Tech

OFFENSIVE LINEMAN

Tre Giller of Southern Methodist (OT)
Chris Reed of Southwestern Missouri (OG)
Eric Wenckowski of Northern Illinois (C)

TIGHT ENDS

Scott Asman of West Chester (Pennsylvania)
Eric Ihnat of Marshall (West Virginia)

FULLBACKS

Tim Cross of Tennessee State
Steve Montgomery of Michigan State

DEFENSIVE LINEMEN

Patrick Moore of Cal Poly-SLO (DE)
James Williams of Cheyney State (Pennsylvania) (DT)

But, as Bill Tobin put it, ''By the time this book of yours goes to press, a lot of these guys will not be around.'' And he was quite correct. Of the twelve players drafted, only five actually made the active roster: Stan Thomas, Chris Zorich, Anthony Morgan, Darren Lewis, and Michael Stonebreaker. Two were maintained on injured reserve: Chris Gardocki and Stacy Long. And two were placed on the Bears' practice squad: Paul Justin and Tom Backes. The three who failed to make the team were fourth-rounder Joe Johnson, eighth-rounder Larry Horton, and twelfth-rounder John Cook.

Of the twenty-three free agents, only one found a place on the active roster (defensive tackle James Williams) and only two on the practice squad (tight end Eric Ihnat and wide receiver Eric Wright).

First-round draft pick Stan Thomas fulfilled his prediction: He became a starter during the season—actually the Bears' first game—after veteran offensive left tackle Jim Covert was sidelined for the year with a back injury. Thomas maintained the starting job through the first nine games, but his play was inconsistent and he caused some costly penalties that resulted in him losing the position to five-year veteran John Wojciechowski.

It was disappointing, but not despairingly so. Mike Ditka expressed the opinion that he had never expected Thomas to start during his rookie year. He felt he needed grooming at the position and that it would be a year or two before he would be ready to handle the responsibilities of protecting the Bear passer and opening holes for the team's running backs.

Fifth-round draft pick Anthony Morgan was another starter in the first game of the 1991 regular season, replacing injured wide receiver Ron Morris. He caught two passes for nineteen yards that day and gained another three on an end-around. He started the next five games but gave up his role to Tom Waddle in game six. He ended the season with thirteen receptions for 211 yards and two touchdowns, making him the eighth most productive pass receiver on the team. His eighty-four-yard touchdown pass play against the Colts (he ran seventy-five yards of the way after the nine-yard pass) was the most dazzling play of the season for Bear fans. The Bears are expecting good things from him in the future, especially as a big-play threat.

Chris Zorich served as a backup defensive lineman and saw limited time on the field, during which time he was credited with six tackles. Rookie free agent James Williams served in the same capacity, recording one quarterback sack and fourteen tackles. Michael Stonebreaker saw a few minutes at linebacker, played on special teams, and was responsible for four tackles.

Running back Darren Lewis carried the ball only fifteen times and gained only thirty-six yards, but played well in the last weeks and in the playoff game against Dallas. And Chris Gardocki, who spent most of the season on injured reserve, did play late in the season and handled some of the Bear kickoffs in the last two games of the year—*mis*handled them in the playoff loss to the Cowboys—but did not attempt a field goal, extra point, or punt.

For the Bears, it was not an impact draft like 1940, when rookie George McAfee went on to dazzle the fans with breakaway runs, rookie Bulldog Turner intimidated and beat up opponents on offense and defense, and rookie Ken Kavanaugh snared a slew of Sid Luckman's passes (the team with those three rookies in its starting lineup demolished the Washington Redskins that year in the NFL championship game by the largest score ever recorded in league history, 73–0). Nor were there debuts as in 1965, when rookie Gale Sayers tied an NFL record by scoring six touchdowns in a single game and set a Bear (still-standing) record of twenty-two touchdowns in a single season, and Dick Butkus added a new dimension of ferocity to the position of middle linebacker (both were honored as All-Pros their first season in the NFL).

There were no true impact players to come out of the 1991 NFL draft—no Eric Dickerson, who gained 1,808 yards for the Los Angeles Rams in 1983 to lead the NFL in rushing his rookie year; no Jerry Rice, who dazzled the San Francisco 49er fans as he gathered in spectacular passes from Joe Montana in 1985, averaging almost nineteen yards a catch; no Barry Sanders, who ran for 1,470 yards with a 5.3 average per carry, including an NFL-high fourteen rushing touchdowns, when he made his debut with the Detroit Lions in 1989; no Mark Carrier, who snatched off ten enemy passes in 1990 for the Bears, the most interceptions in the NFL that year.

The only true impact player to come out of the 1991 draft was the one who was not in it—Raghib "Rocket" Ismail. But he made his impact up in Canada.

The Rocket set a Canadian Football League record for the most combined yardage gained in the regular season (rushing, pass receptions, and punt and kickoff returns). He also carried the Toronto Argonauts to the Grey Cup championship game, the equivalent of the NFL's Super Bowl, where they won their first CFL crown since 1983 and only their second since the title game was instituted back in 1954, decisively defeating the Calgary Stampeders, 36–21. Ismail was also named the Grey Cup game's Most Valuable Player.

Overall in the NFL, of the 334 players drafted, only 130 were on the opening day rosters of the teams that drafted them. The number of rookie free agents who managed to don uniforms for one team or another was a mere twenty (which included non-draftees, often from less-than-known colleges, or those draftees cut from other teams). There was also a sprinkling of rookies on injured reserve.

Only twenty-three of the twenty-seven first-round draft choices of 1991 were listed on NFL rosters on opening day of the regular season, the other four missing either because they were on injured reserve or they had not signed contracts. The absentees: Eric Turner (Cleveland Browns), Bruce Pickens (Atlanta Falcons), Eric Swann (Phoenix Cardinals), and Henry Jones (Buffalo Bills).

Of the second-rounders, twenty-four of twenty-eight were in uniform for the first game of the regular season, as were twenty-one of twenty-eight third-rounders, and eighteen of the fourth-rounders. From rounds five through eight, thirty-six of 112 made it, but only eight of 112 were tapped from rounds nine through twelve.

The breakdown by position of those draftees and rookie free agents who were there when the NFL kicked off the 1991 regular season is this:

Defensive backs	25
Wide receivers	22
Running backs	21
Linebackers	19
Defensive tackles	15
Defensive ends	13
Offensive tackles	12
Quarterbacks	7
Tight ends	6
Offensive guards	5
Centers	3
Kickers	2

*   *   *

The Dallas Cowboys and the Tampa Bay Buccaneers had the most rookies on their opening day rosters, eight apiece. Of the remaining ten players the Cowboys drafted (Dallas had the most picks in the 1991 draft), nine did not make the team, and one, first-round choice Kelvin Pritchett, a defensive end, was traded to the Detroit Lions.

The first selection in the draft, the heralded defensive tackle Russell Maryland, did not start on opening day for the Cowboys and viewed games from the sidelines for most of the first half of the season. He became a starter in the ninth game, where he remained the rest of the season, playing quite well. In fact, Dallas coach Jimmy Johnson said Maryland was a significant factor in the Cowboys' five-game winning streak at the end of the year, which enabled Dallas to get into the playoffs. It also enabled Russell Maryland to perform in a playoff game in his hometown, Chicago, because the Cowboys opened the 1991 postseason in a wild-card game against the Bears, which the Cowboys won.

Owner Jerry Jones said of Maryland, "He's a guy who I think exemplifies the team. He was hit hard early [with criticism], but he kept sticking to things he knows how to do. I'm proud of him."

The other Dallas first-rounder, wide receiver Alvin Harper, ended up starting most of the games in the second half of the season and was also considered a contributor to the Cowboys' strong performance during that period. Larry Brown, taken in the twelfth and last round of the draft, turned out to be a true sleeper and one of the best defensive rookies of 1991.

The remaining five players to have made the team (with the round in which they were selected in parentheses) served only as backups: linebacker Godfrey Myles (three), offensive tackle Eric Williams (three), running back Curvin Richards (four), defensive end Tony Hill (four), linebacker Darrick Brownlow (five). Dallas's draft score: eight of eighteen.

*   *   *

The second pick in the 1991 draft, safety Eric Turner, spent most of the first half of the year on injured reserve for the Cleveland Browns. By mid-season, however, Turner was in the starting lineup, performing credibly on an otherwise bad team (6–10–0).

Only five others made the Brown team. Second-rounder guard Ed King toiled on the offensive line all season and was impressive. Defensive tackle James Jones (three) spent most of the year on the bench, but to the consternation of pro football announcers throughout the league, Pio Sagapolutele (four), another defensive tackle, took to the field and made a fine showing. Wide receiver Michael Jackson (six) and defensive tackle Frank Conover (eight) were also backups. Three rookie free agents were present on Cleveland's opening day roster: defensive end Ernie Logan from East Carolina, tight end Bruce McGonnigal of Virginia, and center Chris Thome from Minnesota, none of whom racked up a lot of playing time. Cleveland's draft score: five of eleven, plus three rookie free agents.

Cornerback Bruce Pickens, the surprise third pick, was a total flop for the Atlanta Falcons. He was a holdout and when he finally did sign after the start of the regular season, he arrived fat and out of shape. He ended the season as a third-string defensive back.

On the other hand, Atlanta's second first-round choice, wide receiver Mike Pritchard, had an outstanding rookie season and contributed to the Falcons making the playoffs for the first time since 1982. Pritchard, a starter, caught fifty passes for 624 yards. Quarterback Brett Favre, another second-rounder, threw five passes for Atlanta; unfortunately, the only two he completed were to the opposing team. He was traded to Green Bay in 1992.

Defensive tackle Moe Gardner (four) played very well, and was runner-up to Denver's Mike Croel for the Associated Press award for Defensive Rookie of the Year. The only other draftee, running back Erric Pegram (six), was also a contributor, and in fact carried the ball more than any other Falcon (101 times for 349 yards). Rookie free agent Brad Daluiso handled some kick-offs for the Falcons before they traded him to the Buffalo Bills. Atlanta's draft score: five of fourteen, plus one rookie free agent.

The fourth pick, linebacker Mike Croel, was the closest thing to an impact player to come out of the 1991 draft. He had a fine season for the Denver Broncos, another team that made the play-offs. He was named by the AP as NFL Defensive Rookie of the Year, garnering sixty-eight of the eighty-two votes. Linebacker Keith Traylor (three) proved that a small college (Central State, Oklahoma) was not a drawback and held his own against the NFL vets when he got the chance. Five other draftees made the Bron-cos. One saw a decent amount of playing time, tight end Reggie Johnson (two), but the others were for the most part bench-warmers: wide receiver Derek Russell (four), running back Greg Lewis (five), offensive tackle Nick Subis (six), and defensive end Kenny Walker (eight). Running back Reggie Rivers of Southwest Texas State, a rookie free agent, also made the opening day roster and proved to be a fine special teams player. Denver's draft score was seven of ten, plus one rookie free agent.

The Los Angeles Rams, who had the fifth selection in the '91 draft, had only three draftees and no rookie free agents on the team opening day. The number five pick, cornerback Todd Lyght, made the starting lineup the second half of the season and played up to his potential. The other two draftees to stick were linebacker Roman Phifer (two) and defensive end Robert Young (five). Young made his presence known and got some recognition for it. But actually nobody contributed much to the 3–13–0 Rams. The Rams' draft score: three of eleven.

Perhaps the second-biggest bust after Atlanta's Bruce Pickens was the number six choice, the college-less defensive end Eric

Swann. He began the season on injured reserve, started one game, and was a major disappointment, proving again that Phoenix is a lousy drafting team and that gambles in the first round rarely pay off.

The other defensive end the Cardinals drafted, Mike Jones (two), was also a letdown.

Illustrating that the Cardinals' drafting instincts aren't *all* bad, cornerback Aeneas Williams played exceptionally well for Phoenix and was considered one of the finest rookie defensive players in the league.

Running back Ivory Lee Brown (seven) made his name only on injured reserve, and rookie free agent cornerback Steve Lofton served as a backup.

If the Cardinals cannot draft well, they at least can trade well. At the start of the season they bartered with Miami and came away with the Dolphins' first-round choice, wide receiver Randal Hill, who went on to become the Cardinals' most productive pass catcher in 1991. Phoenix's draft score: four of thirteen, plus one free agent, plus one rookie acquisition by trade.

Tampa Bay took the first of the highly regarded offensive linemen in the '91 draft with the seventh selection, Charles McRae, and the massive tackle, an immediate starter, played very well for a team that did not (it finished at 3–13–0). The Buccaneers are very pleased with him.

They feel the same about wide receiver Lawrence Dawsey (three), who turned out to be one of the best rookie wide receivers in the league, despite the very erratic passing game of the Buccaneers. Tony Covington (four) did quite well at safety when he got the chance.

The remaining five draftees contributed little or nothing to the hapless Bucs: running back Robert Wilson (three), guard Tim Ryan (five), defensive tackle Rhett Hall (six), linebacker Calvin Tiggle (seven), and defensive back Marty Carter (eight).

Tampa picked up three rookie free agents as well, none of whom clocked much playing time: running backs Robert Hardy of the obscure Carson-Newman College (Jefferson City, Tennessee) and Chuck Weatherspoon of Houston, and defensive back Glenn Rogers out of Memphis State. Tampa Bay's draft score: eight of fourteen, plus three free agents.

Antone Davis, who played the other offensive tackle down the line from Charles McRae at Tennessee, followed him in the draft and did not do nearly as well at the beginning of the season, but improved considerably as the games went on. The number eight pick was a big help late for the Philadelphia Eagles, but not enough to get them into the playoffs, even though they ended up with a record of 10–6–0.

Running back James Joseph, a seventh-round pick, ended up a starter at the end of the season and therefore qualifies as a sleeper. The other four draftees to make the team watched the Eagles' games from ringside most of the time: offensive tackle Rob Selby (three), linebacker William Thomas (four), defensive end Andy Harmon (six), and linebacker Scott Kowalkowski (eight). Rookie free agent quarterback Brad Goebel of Baylor started out on the inactive list, then watched quarterbacks Randall Cunningham and Jim McMahon go down with injuries and the acquired Jeff Kemp end up the season signal-calling for Philadelphia. Philadelphia's draft score: six of twelve, plus one free agent.

Stanley Richard, the second safety taken in the draft and the number nine choice, was an instant starter for the San Diego Chargers and looked very good on a team that could win only four of its sixteen games. Guard Eric Moten (two) showed big-league potential when he played and appears to have a good future ahead of him.

Two other draftees who made the team left much to be desired: defensive tackle George Thornton (two), and well-anticipated

177

running back Eric Bieniemy (two), who spent most of his time on injured reserve. The eleventh-round choice, wide receiver Joaquim Weinberg, and rookie free agent Shawn Jefferson of Central Florida, another wide receiver, spent most of their time off the field of play. San Diego's draft score: five of fifteen, plus one free agent.

The Detroit Lions had the tenth choice in 1991, drafted dreadfully, but turned a 6–10–0 season in 1990 into a divisional championship 12–4–0 in '91. Their top pick, wide receiver Herman Moore, was a bust; their next choice, another wide receiver who also just happened to be *the* highest-rated player according to the National Scouting Combine, Reggie Barrett (three), was an even bigger flop.

Defensive end Kelvin Pritchett, who the Lions acquired after the Cowboys took him in the first round, was a winner and a big help in Detroit's quest for its first playoff berth in almost a decade.

The other three draftees to survive the summer cuts and make it to the regular season served as backups on the turn-around Lions: defensive back Kevin Scott (four), guard Scott Conover (five), and running back Cedric Jackson (eight). Detroit's draft score: five of ten, plus, of course, tradee Kelvin Pritchett.

Probably the best draft of the year was registered by the New England Patriots, who traded away the chance to pay megamillion bucks to Rocket Ismail and instead came up with two first-round choices, both of whom were impressive their rookie year in the NFL. Offensive tackle Pat Harlow and running back Leonard Russell made it clear they have the potential of being Pro Bowl players of the future. Russell, the NFL's Offensive Rookie of the Year, rushed for 959 yards in 1991.

Defensive back Jerome Henderson (two) was a disappointment but someone New England has no plans of giving up on. Quarterback Scott Zolak (four), running back Jon Vaughn (five), tight end Ben Coates (five), and defensive back Harry Colon (eight) made it into uniform, as did rookie free agent wide receiver Rob Carpenter of Syracuse (who had originally been drafted by Cincinnati). Vaughn made a mark as a good kickoff return man.

Maybe it was the rookies! The Patriots improved from 1–15–0 in 1990 to 6–10–0 in 1991. Final draft score for New England, the team that had the first draft choice in every round save the first two: seven of fifteen, plus one free agent.

Linebacker Huey Richardson was the fifteenth pick of the draft, and the Pittsburgh Steelers were delighted to land him. Unfortunately, he spent a lot of time on injured reserve and played in only the last four games. Next year will tell for him.

Tight end Adrian Cooper (four) played quite well for the Steelers after injuries sidelined their veteran tight ends. Pittsburgh's other four draftees to make it played backup: wide receivers Jeff Graham (two) and Ernie Mills (three), running back Leroy Thompson (six), and linebacker Jeff Brady (twelve). Two rookie free agents also made the team but saw limited action: defensive backs Kevin Smith of Rhode Island and Shawn Vincent of Akron. Pittsburgh's draft score: six of twelve, plus two free agents.

Dan McGwire was the first quarterback taken when Seattle selected him with the sixteenth pick. He served only as a backup to Dave Krieg. Fourth-round draft choice John Kasay proved to be the best rookie kicker of the year and handled those chores for the Seahawks all season. The only other draftees to make the final cut, wide receivers Doug Thomas (two) and David Daniels (three), were backups. Seattle's draft score: four of nine.

The Washington Redskins ended up with only two new faces on the team opening day, but as it turned out they did not need a real lot of help from newcomers, seeing as how they won fourteen of their sixteen regular-season games, the most they had ever won since the franchise was founded in 1936. First-round draft choice Bobby Wilson was a trustworthy backup at defensive tackle. And running back Ricky Ervins played very well and was considered a definite contributor to the Super Bowl champion Redskins, gaining 680 yards rushing during the regular season. Washington's draft score: two of nine.

Linebacker Alfred Williams, Cincinnati's first-round pick and the eighteenth of the draft, earned a starting position, albeit on one of the worst teams in the NFL (3–13–0). Quarterback Donald Hollas (four) had more playing time than any other rookie quarterback, filling in when Boomer Esiason was out. The only other two draftees to make the Bengals were backups, defensive tackle Lamar Rogers (two) and center Mike Arthur (five). Arthur played often enough and well enough to make the All-Rookie team. Cincinnati's draft score: four of thirteen.

The Green Bay Packers, who fill the needs on their roster mainly from Plan B, uniformed three rookies in 1991. Their first-round choice, cornerback Vince Clark, won a starting position and played very well for a team that did not (4–12–0). The second-round pick, defensive tackle Esera Tuaolo, also saw a lot of playing time and showed definite potential. The only other draftee to make it, defensive end Don Davey, was a backup. Green Bay's draft score: three of fourteen.

The Kansas City Chiefs were another team that suited up only a few rookies. Their first-round draft choice, running back Harvey Williams, ran quite well when he got to play and is considered to have a good future in the NFL. Wide receiver Tim Barnett (three) caught forty-one passes, second most on the team, and was considered a major contributor his rookie year. Offensive tackle Joe Valerio (two) served as a backup on the playoff-bound Chiefs. Kansas City's draft score: three of eleven.

*   *   *

The Miami Dolphins traded away their first choice in the 1991 draft, wide receiver Randal Hill, who ended up playing to mixed reviews with the Phoenix Cardinals. The Dolphins' second-round choice, running back Aaron Craver, from whom a lot of people expected big things, was a letdown.

Fifth-round choice Brian Cox, a linebacker from unheralded Western Illinois, earned high grades for his performance down in Miami. Three backups fill out the Dolphins' rookie contingent: guard Gene Williams (five), cornerback Chris Green (seven), and wide receiver Scott Miller (nine). Miller was the best rookie punt returner in the league. Two rookie free agents also watched from the sidelines, safety Mike Iaquaniello from Michigan State and nose tackle Chuck Klingbeil of Northern Michigan. Miami's draft score: five of ten, plus two rookie free agents.

The Los Angeles Raiders finally exposed their first-round choice in the last game of the regular season. Controversial quarterback Todd Marinovich, the twenty-fourth pick, filled in for injured Jay Schroeder and threw three touchdown passes and completed twenty-three of forty passes in a most impressive debut.

Their second-round selection also did well, running back Nick Bell, who was their second most productive rusher (307 yards) despite being on injured reserve for a good part of the season. Both defensive tackle Nolan Harrison and tight end Andrew Glover saw some playing time, but not much. One rookie free agent, linebacker Michael Jones, served also as a backup. The Raiders' draft score: four of nine, plus one rookie free agent.

The 49ers were expecting a lot from defensive tackle Ted Washington, the twenty-fifth pick in 1991, but he merely filled in as a backup. They did not get much from the next two to make the team, either, linebackers John Johnson (two) and Mitch Donahue (four).

San Francisco's fifth-round selection, Merton Hanks, how-ever, ended up starting at cornerback late in the season. San Francisco's draft score: four of thirteen.

The Buffalo Bills had only one rookie on their opening day roster, second-round pick Phil Hansen, a defensive end, who worked his way to a starting position in some games late in the season. Their first-round choice, cornerback Henry Jones, who had not signed a contract, would not join the squad until later in the season and would remain a backup. Buffalo's draft score: two of eleven.

The last pick in the first round of the 1991 draft, fullback Jarrod Bunch, went to the New York Giants, but he rarely ap-peared on the field of play for them. The other four draftees to make the final cut did not contribute much, either, to the Super Bowl champions of 1990, who fell from grace in '91 and did not even make the playoffs. But linebacker Kanavis McGhee (two), wide receiver Ed McCaffrey (three), offensive tackle Clarence Jones (four), and linebacker Corey Miller (six) are well-regarded by New York general manager George Young, who sees places for all of them in the Giants' future. The Giants' draft score: five of twelve.

Five teams did not have a selection in the first round of the 1991 draft.

The Houston Oilers had three second-rounders, however. Safety Mike Dumas saw a fair amount of playing time and could be a starter in 1992. Cornerback Darryl Lewis served mainly as a backup, as did center John Flannery. Other bench-warmers for the Oilers were cornerback Steve Jackson (three), offensive tackle Kevin Donnalley (three), safety Marcus Robertson (four), and wide receivers Gary Brown (eight) and Alex Johnson (twelve). Houston's draft score: eight of fourteen.

*   *   *

The Indianapolis Colts had a dismal draft, although probably not as dismal as their 1991 season, during which they won only one of sixteen games. Five rookies made the team: defensive end Shane Curry (two), cornerback Dave McCloughan (three), offensive tackle Mark Vander Poel (four), tight end Kerry Cash (five), and defensive tackle Mel Agee (six). None were starters. The Colts' draft score: five of eleven. A tragic footnote: Shane Curry, out of the University of Miami (Florida), the fortieth pick overall in the 1991 draft, would play only one season for the Colts; he was shot and killed during a quarrel in a motel parking lot in Cincinnati in May 1992.

The Minnesota Vikings did not have a selection until the third round. There they took wide receiver Jake Reed, and in the fourth round they chose running back Randy Baldwin. They were the only two to make the squad, and neither had any impact whatsoever. Minnesota's draft score: two of twelve.

The second-round choice of the New Orleans Saints, wide receiver Wesley Carroll, saw a good deal of playing time as the third wide-out on the ball club. The feeling is that he will develop into a first-stringer in the near future. Cornerback Reginald Jones (five) and linebacker Scott Ross (eleven) were backups. New Orleans's draft score: three of eight.

The New York Jets, who had exercised their first-round choice in the 1990 supplemental draft, kept three draftees. From the second round came quarterback Browning Nagle, who threw a total of two passes all season—one of which he completed. Linebacker Morris Lewis (three) looked good enough when he played to earn a slot on the All-Rookie team, while defensive tackle Mark Gunn (four) had only a backup role. The Jets' draft score: three of eleven.

*   *   *

So, at the end of the 1991 season, the NFL scorecard for rookies reads about thirty, maybe thirty-five, contributors for every thousand college might-have-been-pros.

NFL teams vary in their expenditures for scouting and drafting players, ranging from approximately $500,000 a year for the cheapies to as much as $2 million for the big spenders. Most spend around $1 million each year to finance their way to D-Day.

Averaging it out, NFL teams spend about $28 million each year to find 150 or so players who will either entertain us on the field or keep the benches of their respective teams warm.

This, of course, does not include what it costs to *sign* them.

The price of beef in the NFL meat market—unguaranteed, to boot—is indeed high.

APPENDIX A

1. THE BEST

OFFENSIVE ROOKIE OF THE YEAR, 1991:
LEONARD RUSSELL

Running back Russell from Arizona State, drafted by the New England Patriots, the fourteenth pick in the first round of the 1991 draft, was only forty-one yards shy of a thousand-yard rushing season his rookie year and was the fourth most productive rusher in the AFC.

DEFENSIVE ROOKIE OF THE YEAR, 1991:
MIKE CROEL

Linebacker Croel from Nebraska, selected by the Denver Broncos, was the fourth pick in the 1991 draft. He did not move into Denver's starting lineup until the fourth game of the regular season, but by the eleventh game he was leading the AFC in quarterback sacks. He missed three of the Broncos' last four games but still ended up sixth in sacks in the AFC, with ten.

2. 1991 ALL-ROOKIE TEAM

After all the money was spent scouting, drafting, and signing the rookies of 1991, the following are the ones who made an impression in the NFL. According to *Pro Football Weekly*, this is the NFL All-Rookie team of 1991:

Offense

Position	Player	Drafted by	College	Round Selected
WR	Lawrence Dawsey	Tampa Bay	Florida State	3
WR	Mike Pritchard	Atlanta	Colorado	1
TE	Adrian Cooper	Pittsburgh	Oklahoma	4
OT	Pat Harlow	New England	Southern Cal	1
OT	Antone Davis	Philadelphia	Tennessee	1
OG	Ed King	Cleveland	Auburn	2
OG	Eric Moten	San Diego	Michigan State	2
C	Mike Arthur	Cincinnati	Texas A & M	5
QB*	———			
RB	Leonard Russell	New England	Arizona State	1
RB	Ricky Ervins	Washington	Southern Cal	3

Defense

Position	Player	Drafted by	College	Round Selected
DE	Robert Young	LA Rams	Mississippi St.	5
DE	Pio Sagapolutele	Cleveland	San Diego State	4
DT	Russell Maryland	Dallas	Miami (FL)	1
NT	Moe Gardner	Atlanta	Illinois	4
OLB	Mike Croel	Denver	Nebraska	1
OLB	Morris Lewis	NY Jets	Georgia	3
ILB	Keith Traylor	Denver	Central St. (OK)	3
CB	Aeneas Williams	Phoenix	Southern (LA)	3
CB	Larry Brown	Dallas	Texas Christian	12
S	Eric Turner	Cleveland	UCLA	1
S	Tony Covington	Tampa Bay	Virginia	4

Specialists

Position	Player	Drafted by	College	Round Selected
PK	John Kasay	Seattle	Georgia	4
P†	———			
KO-R	Jon Vaughn	New England	Michigan	5
P-R	Scott Miller	Miami	UCLA	9
ST	Reggie Rivers	Denver	Southwest Texas State	RFA††

Key:	PK	Placekicker
	P	Punter
	KO-R	Kickoff returner
	P-R	Punt returner
	ST	Special teams

*Because no quarterback made any impact whatsoever until Todd Marinovich of the Los Angeles Raiders did in the last game of the regular season, *Pro Football Weekly* "felt that one game did not merit All-Rookie honors."
†No NFL team used a rookie punter in the 1991 season.
††Rookie free agent

3. NUMBER ONE DRAFT CHOICES

The following are the number one draft choices each year since the NFL draft was inaugurated in 1936. The American Football League held its own draft from 1961 through 1966 before it merged with the National Football League. The AFL's first choices for that period are also included here.

Year	Number One	College	Drafted by	Years Played in NFL
1936	Jay Berwanger (HB)	Chicago	Philadelphia Eagles (traded to Chicago Bears)	0
1937	Sam Francis (FB)	Nebraska	Philadelphia Eagles (traded to Chicago Bears)	4
1938	Corbett Davis (FB)	Indiana	Cleveland Rams	4
1939	Ki Aldrich (C)	TCU	Chicago Cardinals	7
1940	George Cafego (HB)	Tennessee	Chicago Cardinals (traded to Brooklyn Dodgers)	4

Year	Number One	College	Drafted by	Years Played in NFL
1941	Tom Harmon (HB)	Michigan	Chicago Bears	0
1942	Bill Dudley* (HB)	Virginia	Pittsburgh Steelers	8
1943	Frank Sinkwich (HB)	Georgia	Detroit Lions	3
1944	Angelo Bertelli (QB)	Notre Dame	Boston Yanks	0
1945	Charley Trippi* (HB)	Georgia	Chicago Cardinals	9
1946	Frank Dancewicz (QB)	Notre Dame	Boston Yanks	3
1947	Bob Fenimore (HB)	Oklahoma A & M	Chicago Bears	1
1948	Harry Gilmer (QB)	Alabama	Washington Redskins	8
1949	Chuck Bednarik* (C)	Pennsylvania	Philadelphia Eagles	14
1950	Leon Hart (E)	Notre Dame	Detroit Lions	8
1951	Kyle Rote (HB)	SMU	New York Giants	11
1952	Bill Wade (QB)	Vanderbilt	Los Angeles Rams	13
1953	Harry Babcock (E)	Georgia	San Francisco 49ers	3
1954	Bobby Garrett (QB)	Stanford	Cleveland Browns	1
1955	George Shaw (QB)	Oregon	Baltimore Colts	8
1956	Gary Glick (DB)	Colorado A & M	Pittsburgh Steelers	7
1957	Paul Hornung* (QB)	Notre Dame	Green Bay Packers	9

Year	Number One	College	Drafted by	Years Played in NFL
1958	King Hill (QB)	Rice	Chicago Cardinals	12
1959	Randy Duncan (QB)	Iowa	Green Bay Packers	1
1960	Billy Cannon (HB)	LSU	Los Angeles Rams	11
1961				
NFL	Tommy Mason (HB)	Tulane	Minnesota Vikings	12
AFL	Ken Rice (G)	Auburn	Buffalo Bills	6
1962				
NFL	Ernie Davis (HB)	Syracuse	Washington Redskins	0
AFL	Roman Gabriel (QB)	NC State	Oakland Raiders	16
1963				
NFL	Terry Baker (QB)	Oregon State	Los Angeles Rams	3
AFL	Buck Buchanan (DT)	Grambling	Kansas City Chiefs	13
1964				
NFL	Dave Parks (WR)	Texas Tech	San Francisco 49ers	9
AFL	Jack Concannon (QB)	Boston College	Boston Patriots	11
1965				
NFL	Tucker Frederickson (HB)	Auburn	New York Giants	6
AFL	Lawrence Elkins (WR)	Baylor	Houston Oilers	2
1966				
NFL	Tommy Nobis (LB)	Texas	Atlanta Falcons	11

Year	Number One	College	Drafted by	Years Played in NFL
AFL	Jim Grabowski (FB)	Illinois	Miami Dolphins	6
1967	Bubba Smith (DT)	Michigan State	Baltimore Colts	9
1968	Ron Yary (T)	Southern Cal	Minnestoa Vikings	15
1969	O. J. Simpson* (RB)	Southern Cal	Buffalo Bills	11
1970	Terry Bradshaw* (QB)	Louisiana Tech	Pittsburgh Steelers	14
1971	Jim Plunkett (QB)	Stanford	New England Patriots	15
1972	Walt Patulski (DE)	Notre Dame	Buffalo Bills	5
1973	John Matuszak (DE)	Tampa	Houston Oilers	10
1974	Ed Jones (DE)	Tennessee State	Dallas Cowboys	11
1975	Steve Bartkowski (QB)	California	Atlanta Falcons	11
1976	Lee Roy Selmon (DE)	Oklahoma	Tampa Bay Buccaneers	9
1977	Ricky Bell (RB)	Southern Cal	Tampa Bay Buccaneers	9
1978	Earl Campbell* (RB)	Texas	Houston Oilers	8
1979	Tom Cousineau (LB)	Ohio State	Buffalo Bills	4
1980	Billy Sims (RB)	Oklahoma	Detroit Lions	5

Year	Number One	College	Drafted by	Years Played in NFL
1981	George Rogers (RB)	South Carolina	New Orleans Saints	5
1982	Ken Sims (DT)	Texas	New England Patriots	4
1983	John Elway (QB)	Stanford	Baltimore Colts (traded to Denver Broncos)	†
1984	Irving Fryar (WR)	Nebraska	New England Patriots	†
1985	Bruce Smith (DE)	Virginia Tech	Buffalo Bills	†
1986	Bo Jackson (RB)	Auburn	Tampa Bay Buccaneers	4
1987	Vinny Testaverde (QB)	Miami (FL)	Tampa Bay Buccaneers	†
1988	Aundray Bruce (LB)	Alabama	Atlanta Falcons	†
1989	Troy Aikman (QB)	UCLA	Dallas Cowboys	†
1990	Jeff George (QB)	Illinois	Indianapolis Colts	†
1991	Russell Maryland (DT)	Miami (FL)	Dallas Cowboys	†

*Made it to the Pro Football Hall of Fame
†Still an active player in the NFL

4. FIRST PICKS BY POSITION (THROUGH 1991)

Quarterback	19
Running Back/Halfback	18
Wide Receiver/End	5
Defensive End	5
Defensive Tackle	4
Fullback	3
Linebacker	3
Center	2
Defensive Back	1
Offensive Guard	1
Offensive Tackle	1

5. FIRST PICKS BY COLLEGE (THROUGH 1991)

College	Number
Notre Dame	5
Auburn	4
Georgia	3
Southern Cal	3
Stanford	3
Texas	3
Illinois	2
Miami (Florida)	2
Nebraska	2
Oklahoma	2

All the following have contributed one player each:
Alabama
Baylor
Boston College
California

Chicago
Colorado A & M
Grambling
Indiana
Iowa
Louisiana State
Louisiana Tech
Michigan
Michigan State
North Carolina State
Ohio State
Oklahoma A & M
Oregon
Oregon State
Pennsylvania
Rice
South Carolina
Southern Methodist
Syracuse
Tampa
Tennessee
Tennessee State
Texas Christian
Texas Tech
Tulane
UCLA
Vanderbilt
Virginia
Virginia Tech

6. NFL/AFL TEAMS THAT HAVE HAD THE FIRST PICK

Team	Number of Times
Buffalo Bills	5
Baltimore/Indianapolis Colts	4
Boston/New England Patriots	4
Chicago/St. Louis/Phoenix Cardinals	4
Cleveland/Los Angeles Rams	4
Tampa Bay Buccaneers	4
Atlanta Falcons	3
Dallas Cowboys	3
Detroit Lions	3
Houston Oilers	3
Philadelphia Eagles	3
Pittsburgh Steelers	3
Boston Yanks	2
Chicago Bears	2
Green Bay Packers	2

Team	Number of Times
Minnesota Vikings	2
New York Giants	2
Oakland/Los Angeles Raiders	2
San Francisco 49ers	2
Washington Redskins	2
Cleveland Browns	1
Kansas City Chiefs	1
Miami Dolphins	1
New Orleans Saints	1

The following teams have never had the first pick in the draft (all are in the AFC):

Cincinnati Bengals
Denver Broncos
New York Jets
San Diego Chargers
Seattle Seahawks

1. 1991 CHICAGO BEAR DRAFTEES AND ROOKIE FREE AGENTS

	Draftee	College	Hometown
1	Stan Thomas	Texas	El Centro, TX
2	Chris Zorich	Notre Dame	Chicago, IL
3	Chris Gardocki	Clemson	Stone Mountain, GA
4	Joe Johnson	North Carolina St.	Hackensack, NJ
5	Anthony Morgan	Tennessee	Cleveland, OH
6	Darren Lewis	Texas A & M	Dallas, TX
7	Paul Justin	Arizona State	Schaumburg, IL (suburb of Chicago)
8	Larry Horton	Texas A & M	Tatum, TX
9	Michael Stonebreaker	Notre Dame	River Ridge, LA
10	Tom Backes	Oklahoma	El Paso, TX
11	Stacy Long	Clemson	Griffin, GA
12	John Cook	Washington	Olympia, WA

Free Agent	College	Hometown
Scott Asman	West Chester (PA)	Bensalem, PA
Sean Becton	Central Florida	Ormond Beach, FL
Richard Booker	Texas Christian	McGregor, TX
Peter Brantley	Oregon	Irvine, CA
Steve Brown	Wake Forest	Washington, DC
Nigel Codrington	Rice	Baytown, TX
Tim Cross	Tennessee State	Clarksville, TN
Anthony Cummings	Louisville	Detroit, MI
Ron Ferguson	Texas Tech	Clements, TX
Tre Giller	Southern Methodist	Richardson, TX
John Hardy	California	Pasadena, CA
Eric Ihnat	Marshall (WV)	Columbus, OH
Michael Johnson	Cal. St./Sacramento	Fairfield, CA
Tim Lance	Eastern Illinois	Cuba, IL
Steve Montgomery	Michigan State	Red Bank, NJ
Patrick Moore	Cal Poly State (San Luis Obispo, CA)	Gresham, OR
Quintin Parker	Illinois	Webster Groves, MO (suburb of St. Louis)
Chris Reed	SW Missouri	Hillsboro, MO
Charles Rowe	Texas Tech	Killeen, TX
Eric Wenckowski	Northern Illinois	Franklin Park, IL (suburb of Chicago)
John Wiley	Auburn	Opelika, AL
James Williams	Cheyney State (PA)	Allerdice, PA
Eric Wright	Stephen F. Austin (TX)	Pittsburgh, TX

2. HOW THE 1991 BEARS WERE BUILT

The following chart is ample testimony to the way in which the Bears rely upon the draft.

Year	Draft	Round Selected	Free Agents	Trade
1991	Stan Thomas (T)	1	John Hardy	Eric
	Chris Zorich (DT)	2	(DB)	Kumerow
	Chris Gardocki (K/P)	3	James Williams	(DE)
	Anthony Morgan (WR)	5	(DT)	
	Darren Lewis (RB)	6		
	Michael Stonebreaker (LB)	9		
	Stacy Long (G)	11		
1990	Mark Carrier (DB)	1		
	Ron Cox (LB)	2		
	Tim Ryan (DT)	3		
	Peter Tom Willis (QB)	3		

Year	Draft	Round Selected	Free Agents	Trade
	John Mangum (DB)	6		
	James Rouse (FB)	8		
	Johnny Bailey (RB)	9		
1989	Trace Armstrong (DE)	1	Maury Buford (P)	
	Donnell Woolford (DB)	1	Tom Waddle (WR)	
	John Roper (LB)	2		
	Jerry Fontenot (C)	3		
	Markus Paul (DB)	4		
	Mark Green (RB)	5		
1988	Brad Muster (FB)	1	Mickey Pruitt (LB)	
	Wendell Davis (WR)	1		
	Dante Jones (LB)	2		
	Jim Thornton (TE)	4		
	Lemuel Stinson (DB)	6		
	David Tate (DB)	8		
1987	Jim Harbaugh (QB)	1	Cap Boso (TE)	
	Ron Morris (WR)	2	John Wojciechowski (G)	
1986	Neal Anderson (RB)	1		
	Maurice Douglass (DB)	8		
	Glen Kozlowski (WR)	11		
1985	William Perry (DT)	1		
	Kevin Butler (K)	4		
	Jim Morrissey (LB)	11		

Year	Draft	Round Selected	Free Agents	Trade
1984	Ron Rivera (LB)	2		
	Shaun Gayle (DB)	10		
1983	Jim Covert (T)	1		
	Tom Thayer (G)	4		
	Richard Dent (DE)	8		
	Mark Bortz (G)	8		
1982	Dennis Gentry (WR)	4		
1981	Keith Van Horne (T)	1	Jay Hilgenberg	
	Mike Singletary (LB)	2	(C)	
			Steve McMichael (DT)	

3. CHICAGO BEARS FIRST-ROUND PICKS

Year	Player	Position	College
1936	Joe Stydahar*	T	West Virginia
1937	Les McDonald	E	Nebraska
1938	Joe Gray	B	Oregon State
1939	Sid Luckman*	QB	Columbia
	Bill Osmanski	B	Holy Cross
1940	Bulldog Turner*	C	Hardin-Simmons
	George McAfee*	B	Duke
1941	Tom Harmon†	B	Michigan
1942	Frankie Albert†	QB	Stanford
1943	Bob Steuber	B	Missouri
1944	Ray Evans†	B	Kansas
1945	Don Lund†	B	Michigan
1946	Johnny Lujack	QB	Notre Dame
1947	Bob Fenimore	B	Oklahoma State
	Don Kindt	B	Wisconsin
1948	Bobby Layne*	QB	Texas
	Max Baumgartner	E	Texas
1949	Dick Harris†	C	Texas

Year	Player	Position	College
1950	Chuck Hunsinger	B	Florida
	Fred Morrison	B	Ohio State
1951	Bob Williams	QB	Notre Dame
	Billy Stone	B	Bradley
1952	Jim Dooley	B	Miami (FL)
1953	Billy Anderson	B	Compton JC
1954	Stan Wallace	B	Illinois
1955	Ron Drzewiecki	B	Marquette
1956	Tex Schriewer†	E	Texas
1957	Earl Leggett	T	Louisiana State
1958	Chuck Howley	G	West Virginia
1959	Don Clark†	B	Ohio State
1960	Roger Davis	G	Syracuse
1961	Mike Ditka*	TE	Pittsburgh
1962	Ronnie Bull	B	Baylor
1963	Dave Behrman†	C	Michigan State
1964	Dick Evey	T	Tennessee
1965	Dick Butkus*	LB	Illinois
	Gale Sayers*	B	Kansas
	Steve DeLong	T	Tennessee
1966	George Rice†	T	Louisiana State
1967	Loyd Phillips	DE	Arkansas
1968	Mike Hull	B	Southern California
1969	Rufus Mayes	T	Ohio State
1970	———— (Choice to Green Bay)		
1971	Joe Moore	B	Missouri
1972	Lionel Antoine	T	Southern Illinois
	Craig Clemons	DB	Iowa
1973	Wally Chambers	DE	Eastern Kentucky
1974	Waymond Bryant	LB	Tennessee State
	Dave Gallagher	DE	Michigan

Year	Player	Position	College
1975	Walter Payton	B	Jackson State
1976	Dennis Lick	T	Wisconsin
1977	Ted Albrecht	T	California
1978	——— (Choice to LA Rams through Cleveland)		
1979	Dan Hampton	DT	Arkansas
	Al Harris	DE	Arizona State
1980	Otis Wilson	LB	Louisville
1981	Keith Van Horne	T	Southern California
1982	Jim McMahon	QB	Brigham Young
1983	Jim Covert	T	Pittsburgh
	Willie Gault	WR	Tennessee
1984	Wilber Marshall	LB	Florida
1985	William Perry	DT	Clemson
1986	Neal Anderson	B	Florida
1987	Jim Harbaugh	QB	Michigan
1988	Brad Muster	B	Stanford
	Wendell Davis	WR	Louisiana State
1989	Donnell Woolford	DB	Clemson
	Trace Armstrong	DE	Florida
1990	Mark Carrier	DB	Southern California
1991	Stan Thomas	T	Texas

*Enshrined in the Pro Football Hall of Fame
†Did not sign with the Bears

4. BEAR SLEEPERS WHO MADE IT

Year	Player	Position	College	Round Selected
1936	Danny Fortmann	G	Colgate	9
1939	Ray Bray	G	Western Michigan	7
1940	Scooter McLean	B	St. Anselm	19
1949	George Blanda	QB	Kentucky	12
1952	Joe Fortunato	LB	Mississippi State	7
	Bill Bishop	T	North Texas State	8
1953	Larry Strickland	C	North Texas State	13
1954	Harlon Hill	WR	North Alabama	15
1956	J. C. Caroline	B	Illinois	7
1957	Bob Kilcullen	T	Texas Tech	8
1958	Johnny Morris	WR	Cal/Santa Barbara	12
1959	Roger LeClerc	K	Trinity (CT)	15
1960	Bo Farrington	WR	Prairie View A & M	16
1961	Mike Pyle	C	Yale	7
1962	Ed O'Bradovich	DE	Illinois	7

Year	Player	Position	College	Round Selected
1965	Dick Gordon	WR	Michigan State	7
	Frank Cornish	DT	Grambling	11
	Ralph Kurek	B	Wisconsin	20
1968	Willie Holman	DE	South Carolina St.	7
1972	Jim Osborne	DT	Southern	7
1975	Doug Plank	DB	Ohio State	12
	Roland Harper	B	Louisiana Tech	17
1976	Jerry Muckenstrum	LB	Arkansas State	7
1983	Richard Dent	DE	Tennessee State	8
	Mark Bortz	G	Iowa	8
1984	Shaun Gayle	DB	Ohio State	10
1985	Jim Morrissey	LB	Michigan State	11

Index